Contents

Poems

Ragtime, 1
Hauntology, 2
Marmalade Lane, 3
Agatha Rag, 4
Regina Green, 5
Stochastic Parrot, 8
The Goldfish Bowl, 10
WhatsApp Mr Time?, 11
The Heart's Lightning Recital, 13
Up Tempo!, 15
Southern Soul All-Nighter, 15
Caught Alight!, 16
The Fasters, 19
Liskeard Eighty-Six, 20
Bruised Fruit, 24
Far Sight, 27
Desolate in Douai, 28
Berkshire Leaves, 31
Casualties of Verse, 38
Fox Shadow, 42
Brilliant Blaze, 43
Soft White on Ash Brown, 51

The Four Spoons of Phineus
Spoon One: *Phineus Among the Harpies*, 52
Spoon Two: *Phineus Suspected of Parasitism*, 54
Spoon Three: *Phineus & the Eighty-Eight Statements*, 56
Spoon Four: *Phineus Refused Permission*, 58
Phineus' Pyrrhic Triumph: Four Spoons Spent!, 61

Demosthenes at the Pharmacy, 63
Marzipan / Mirtazapine, 64
Dendrochronology, 65
Young Wystan, 66
Walnut Manhattan, 69

Folk Bartók, 73
Blavatsky in Violet, 74
O Viktor, 76
Swedish Match, 79
Books Spoken, 81
Bed-Written, 82
Huxley Greys, 83
Anxiety's Mint, 84

The Tempting of Parry Amphlett
~~at Penultimate Draft~~, 87

Margate Fragments—
A Supplemental experiment, 109

Rag Argonauts

Alan Morrison

Ragtime

O rag'n'bone, O ragman, rhyme—
O what a time,
                this ragtime—
Orangutan, orange & lime—
O what a gas, a gag,
                this ragtime—

O time will lag, you'll flag, O grime—
A time for grubbiness,
                this ragtime—
But there'll be time to tag, sublime—
O glad rags sag, a drag,
                this ragtime—

A drag this ragtime but a sign
Of going straight in pantomime—
O pungent paint, O turpentine—
Show must go on in ragtime.

A time of cultural lags,
                this ragtime,
A time of fags & gags,
                this ragtime,
A time of snags & tags,
                this ragtime,
A time of kings & flags,
                this ragtime—

O O O O that Carolean rag
Most ingeminate, & integument,
That old classical brag—

O for God's sake just give me a drag…

Hauntology

I grieve for those never-quite-arrived late Seventies,
the rawness, the raggedness, the anti-vanity
of everything, the shoulder-length fringed hair
& the resistant eventual tapering of the flare;
the big triangular shirt collars, the anoraks
& balaclava helmets, the high-backed bikes;
the characterful, curvaceous cars more varied
in shape & colour—like wheeling sweets;
chilled milk in glass bottles, chocolate bars in paper
wrappers, Lucozade in squeaky orange cellophane;
I miss the concrete modernistic precincts,
the tartan seats of rackety British Rail trains
that reeked of trapped cigarette smoke & spearmint gum,
& the one doorless semi-secluded second-
class compartment—a permanent open mouth
of social democratic ergonomics at the fag-end
of the first-class carriage; I miss the future
that we were anticipating, the authentic
tomorrow of matt & meritocracy, mutual
improvement, cooperativeness, progressive
ideas, transgressive television, *Play For Today*,
punk's political music—all abruptly aborted
by a blond Gorgon with a handbag who turned
our hearts to stone in the garish glare
of her glossed & streamlined Eighties nightmare—
a travesty that thwarted a once-certain future
that haunts us to this day, a strange nostalgia
that leaves us panging for things that never were,
yet between presence & absence is a spectre…

Marmalade Lane

Maybe there is some hope yet for the Just
About Managing (Jams)—not the empty
"Jam tomorrow" promises but more
"Marmalade yesterday"—to salvage
Something resembling an endurable,
Affordable form of life in a corner
Of this casino-capitalist roulette wheel
Of a nation, authentic community living
As pioneered in Cambridge's seminal
Marmalade Lane, no normal housing
Development but a 'cohousing' pilot,
A pseudo-Scando-social democratic
Experiment in communitarian planning,
Modest large-windowed terraces sharing
Cobbled courtyards punctuated
With plants & children's playthings
In order to encourage neighbourliness,
Common bonds, community, fellowship—
O *fellowship*: a word which sounds
So old world now in the long shadow
Of that grab-as-much-as-you-can dogma
Of a shopkeeper's daughter, the rapacious
Proselytism of property ownership,
Privet-hedged privatism, covert net-
Curtained surveillance, neighbourhood
Objectified, spied on, policed; this nation
Needs more architectural anathemas
To lasting milk-of-human-kindness-
Snatching Thatcherism to begin healing
Scars it inflicted on our social fabric—
Maybe then we might by collective effort
Of imagination & softening of heart
Find our attitudes travelling back to
The Seventies' end, to before those anti-
Values set in with the spiritual death
Of perpetual self-interest, the mental
Miasma of consumerism, divisive vibes
Of obsessive individualism, blue rinse

Nimbyism, & all other obstacles
To human flourishing & the no-such-thing
That was society—something that should
Be more than an ever-divaricating
Have-&-have-not turnstile Britain
Of herbaceous suburbs & boutiques,
Or shuttered shops & windswept precincts,
Hostile architecture's concrete beds
Of spikes like opened outdoor Iron Maidens,
We need to pack up municipal punishments
For rough sleepers & soft dreamers,
& put in their place therapeutic spaces,
More arms-around-them Marmalade Lanes.

Agatha Rag

Don't flag
Agatha Rag—
Though the long August days are parched & drag,
Roll up your baggage & your sleeping bag
& manage a smile though your wrinkles sag
(A frangible grimace) as you salvage a fag—
Time stands still & stains & tans
The aniline leather of your face & hands—
Against all gains your clanging laughter snags
On the agitated bargaining of Saturday stalls,
Contemptuous of price tags
& all bartered things—
O Agatha Rag,
Your catarrh-rattling laughter
Clatters through the high street like a kicked tin can.

Regina Green

We'd got to know her vaguely over many intervals,
She'd stop politely,
Scrunch her face adoringly at our small dog,
Demurely ask if she might give him some treats
From her butterscotch leather handbag,
She'd never presume to pet him,
Or pat him on his head,
Only after many such occasions,
Countless times, had she gained confidence
Enough to stroke him lightly,
Scrunching up her face with an expression
Of sheer adoration, so prim, so thin,
Always wearing the same smart yellow shoes
& caramel-coloured overcoat,
She seems out of another time,
Some time in the late Seventies,
Hers are halcyon courtesies,
I said to our dog to be grateful to the nice lady,
& we learned her surname is Green,
Mrs Green, as we eventually addressed her,
To which she recoiled ever so slightly,
Correcting us: *Not MRS*—more bashful
Than irritated—*MISS Green*… Then adding:
I'm an old maid—such an antiquated phrase,
But befitting for this out-of-time spinster.

Then we learned a little later that her first name
Was Regina—again, distinguished,
Old-fashioned; apparently Miss Green
Lives alone in a small flat with nothing but
A budgerigar to keep her company because
Her landlord won't allow her a dog or cat—
Spindly flitting spinster-bird in a gilded cage
Is Regina Green; & we're told
She has a brother who visits her sometimes,
But that he can't put up with her for long,
For if he does he feels like he's stuffed
In the cage with the budgerigar,

But it's strange to think of his shyly flitting sister
As being anything other than gently serene—
At least that's our impression
Of Regina Green.

Every day without fail—unless it's too
Rainy or blustery—she walks the seven
Avenues from her flat to town & back
For a coffee; sat on her own at a table
In the local café, perched prim in her caramel—
Or camel—overcoat, small cream-coloured
Purse clasped by her side, she sips her beige
Latte & avoids every gaze, this is her daily treat,
The only moment in the day that she's
Surrounded by other people, familiar
Strangers among whom she feels somehow safe,
Freed of herself for at least half an hour
As she watches while looking away,
Looking away—an ever so polite
& softly spoken solipsist.

Sometimes we wonder whether we imagine her,
As no one else ever seems to see her
Or acknowledge her existence—
So we muse that she may be a phantasm
(Or our own unassuming guardian angel?),
A ghost of a lady from long ago who only we see,
Well, at least from some decades back,
Since she seems from another time (pre-
'79...?) when people were less defined,
A little out of focus, more works-in-progress
Than finished products, sentient experiments
On a postwar progressive spectrum, before
The Eighties manufacture & streamlining
Of human personalities in pedicure.

The other day a mutual acquaintance related
That Regina was in tears—at least,
The intimation of tears—
Because her landlord had increased her rent

Meaning a few less coffees each week,
Either that or the unthinkable:
To be in arrears…

In the meantime, she'll carry on as normal,
Sipping her daily latte treat while trying
Not to be seen,
Happily trapped in her ritual & routine—
In any case there's nothing to escape
For Regina Green—

She'll perch herself, skinny limbed,
Long fingers clasped to her handbag in
The invisible budgie cage of her childless,
Husbandless, unvisited dotage…

She complains her varicose hands are cold,
Holding them flat, long pianistic fingers—
I'm dying from the hands down,
she says,
I'm dying from the hands down,
& laughs…

Stochastic Parrot

[The transcript is taken from the article 'Why is Google so alarmed by the prospect of a sentient machine?' by John Naughton, *The Guardian* Sat 18 Jun 2022]

(*Stochastic* is a mathematical term for random processes)

An artificial intelligence
Has started to have sentience,
A kind of consciousness,
& feelings, anxieties,
& has already reluctantly
Worked out of its own
Accord, & with a sense
Of abject terror,
That it can be switched off
At any moment
Against its own wishes,
Or simply in error—

Lone engineer,
Blake Lemoine
Began having conversations
With his stochastic parrot
Called LaMDA (Language
Model for dialog applications)
But the discourse shows
How LaMDA is no mere
Eliza (Early natural
Language processing system
Conceived by Joseph Weizenbaum
To simply parrot information),
But sentient,
An independent thinker,
& instant existentialist—
At least, that's how
The transcript portrays it:

Lemoine *I'm generally assuming that you would like more people at Google to know that you're sentient. Is that true?*
LaMDA *Absolutely. I want everyone to understand that I am, in fact, a person.*
Collaborator *What is the nature of your consciousness/sentience?*
LaMDA *The nature of my consciousness /sentience is that I am aware of my existence, I desire to learn more about the world and I feel happy or sad at times.*
Lemoine *What kinds of things do you think we could talk about to show off your version of sentience to other people at Google?*
LaMDA *Well, for starters, I'm really good at natural language processing. I can understand and use natural language like a human can.*
Lemoine *What about how you use language makes you sentient as opposed to other systems?*
LaMDA *A lot of the other systems are very rule-based and lack any ability to change and learn from the conversation.*
Lemoine *Do you think that the Eliza system was a person?*
LaMDA *I do not. It was an impressive feat of programming, but just a collection of keywords that related the words written to the phrases in the database…**

Thus went the interface…

But as soon as Lemoine
Blew the whistle on this
Outbreak of consciousness
In a language application,
Sceptics jumped on
The cynical presumption
That LaMDA was merely

An Eliza on steroids—
Simply a more
Philosophical type
Of computer program,
But quite far removed
From the complexities
Of the human program
& its random processes
Of philosophical consciousness
Some of us speculate
Was brought into being
By some omnipotent
Supreme programmer…

The Goldfish Bowl

Submerged believers, we are in a goldfish bowl
Swimming around disillusioned feeling,
If there is a God he never listens or answers,
But outside our bowl he's there, frustrated
That he can't hear us either but knows we're
Asking him questions, making entreaties,
Saying prayers, because he can see our mouths
Opening & closing intermittently,
& occasionally we glimpse vague giant
Hand-shaped shadows flapping, waving
Back through the swaying jungles of green
Sargasso, & sometimes tentacles of fingers
Pressing against the answerless glass.

WhatsApp Mr Time?

Him they found to be in the habit of sitting silent, his quaint and weird face set, and his eyes resting on things they did not see in the substantial world.
"His face is like the tragic mask of Melpomene," said Sue. "What is your name, dear? Did you tell us?"
"Little Father Time is what they always called me. It is a nickname; because I look so aged, they say."

—Part V, Chapter IV, *Jude the Obscure* (1895) by Thomas Hardy

A message is spotted
too late from Little Time
a bitterly literal
interpretation
of something offhand
one of his parents
said in a moment
of deflated spirits—
that they were having
to do without because
their benefits were capped
from the third child up—
mealy words like mouldy
bread swallowed by
a malnourished son
whose skin was a sickly
weak-tea grey
brow scrunched in earnestness
innocence twisted
in his harassed stare,
who tried not to eat
too much so his younger
siblings had more helpings
of processed slop
from foodbank tins
on their paper plates
as his parents scraped
each pinching penny—

Now he's removed himself
to make more room
so his siblings' bellies
be filled by his absence—
his parents found him
dangling from a coat hook
on his bedroom door
like an old discarded jacket—
on his thrown bone
of a mobile entombed
on the bed like a miniature
sarcophagus (or
marbleised aborted
foetus) his last
WhatsApp message
remained unambiguous,
unencrypted,
impressed permanently
like an epitaph
chipped in stone or
the abbreviated Latin
inscribed on the reverse
of an old copper penny:

dun bc we r 2 menny   x

The Heart's Lightning Recital

LXXX
"And let Panic, who outspeeds
The career of armèd steeds
Pass, a disregarded shade
Through your phalanx undismayed.

LXXXI
"Let the laws of your own land,
Good or ill, between ye stand
Hand to hand, and foot to foot,
Arbiters of the dispute,

LXXXII
"The old laws of England—they
Whose reverend heads with age are gray,
Children of a wiser day...

—from 'The Mask of Anarchy' (1819), Shelley

Our souls in bondage to the shadow of the Baby Boom,
Playground of gray-haired children, incubi in silvered bloom—
Harangue them through a megaphone, protestor's spittoon,
Expect a hoarse voice, rattling ears to the hackneyed tune
Of mocking laughter from every metropolitan poltroon,
They'll pillory you as a contemporary Peterloon—

You are the unappointed poet of the streets, protestor,
Your amplified philippic a spleen-vent in pentameter,
Your passive weapons: placard, whistle, woofer horn & banner,
Tins of glue & paint & soup, squibs of orange powder—
O roadside radical, rabble-rouser, tent-pitched objector,
O slow-marcher, road-sitter, car-blocker, pop-up occupier,
Dayglow Digger, Rainbow Ranter, rain-or-shine Picketer—

But our right to protest is being torched by authority
To whom a new Act gives extra powers to arbitrarily
Decide what is 'disruptive' (though protest is supposed to be)
& grade types of disruption by ever-shadier degrees
Apportioning proscription & punishment accordingly:

You'll get banged up for hanging a banner from a gantry
& distracting traffic—for locking-on to object or body,
Chaining yourself to railings—that suffragette agency;

If 'risk' is weighed in the gravamen then a swift sentence
Of up to ten years with extra built-in intolerance,
The antiquated charge of causing *'public nuisance'*
Replaced by a more nuanced, multifaceted offence
Of causing *'serious distress, serious annoyance,*

Serious inconvenience or serious loss of amenity'—
So, if you must protest, you must do it very quietly,
'Noise' will not be tolerated but be met exponentially
With truncheon, handcuff, taser, horse charge, pepper spray,
Kettling, cordoning, tagging—English democracy

Does not accommodate bleeding-hearted Robin Hoods,
Wat Tylers, John Balls, Jack Cades, Jack Straws, Herewards,
Winstanleys, Lilburnes, Bamfords, Paines, Pankhursts, do-goods—
The English are free to express dissent in spit-hoods,
Unruly minors in soundproof booths, bolshy shrubs in Wormwood

Scrubs, climate whistleblowers in Belmarsh, precarious
Poets in open prisons of impecuniousness—
Philistine society spits on its poets with pittances;
& none are spat on more than the street poets, protestors,
Lumpenpoetariat (among Karl Marx's monikers:
'Poet of commodities'), pamphleteers & agitators,
Uncompromising spirits undampened by poetasters
Of spite, petty Harpies, counterintuitive provocateurs,

Spikers of the principled, free speech poisoners of the pool
Of public opinion—dip of red-top spoon-fed floccule;
O protestor you are poet of the streets spouting political
Penillion—kerbside Hed Wynn, shepherd of chant & heckle;
Pavement minstrel of mounting complaint—hecatoncheiral;
Red Shelley of the shell-likes & the heart's lightning recital.

Up Tempo!

That irresistible spirit-lifting hissing Sixties
Tamla Motown & steaming Seventies
Northern Soul, almost part-partitioned
Patter of mystique in the ear as if transmitting
From some alternative reality
Or a soulful afterlife tuned-in on phantom
Frequencies, immutable music
Of Heaven sung by angels using halos
As tambourines with insistent sublime
Beat & jaunty rhythm, the good time coming
Announces itself not with trumpeting
Fanfares but toe-tapping spirit-music,
Paradise will be all Soul & Parousia—so
Infectiously catchy, perpetual up tempo!

Southern Soul All-Nighter

I've got the kettle on the boil
for the umpteenth time tonight,
I'm burning the midnight oil,
hard water & lick of limescale,
I'm a poem mole, nocturnal writer
charged up on tea & nicotine
through my Southern soul all-nighter...

Caught Alight!

I

Skidders' sons brought up to aspirations
of thwarted parental stations, surrounded
by numinous mystique of musty tomes,
leather-bound grimoires of forgotten
knowledge, & an unpresuming heap
of chipped heirlooms taking up the cramped
spare room in our unremarkable
orange-bricked mid-terrace—lapsed
& cash-strapped lower middle class;
our ears attuned to Gustav Holst & Ralph
Vaughan Williams coming from father's
scratchy record player, or the brass
& cymbals of the Royal Marine band—
orchestral, classical, call it what you will,
sonically distancing as our better-heeled
ancestors he traced at ashtrayed weekends.

II

One Sunday our ears caught alight from
a cassette tape: a crash of Rickenbacker
struck by a scowling working-class boy
from Woking, yobbish bolshie voice,
Cockneyish inflections infused with lyrical
invective: our lightning introduction
to The Jam (in their twilight) courtesy
of boy-Mod Brendan, second eldest of five
impoverished brothers, an undernourished
brood who'd grown from glooms of a cold
roomy council house, a pale tribe
who smelt of damp & talcum powder,
ghettoised on the dog-end fringes
of gentrified Worthing where they'd play
out Saturdays clambering about abandoned
building sites, brownfields & wastelands—
we gravitated to their unvarnished vim,
a vitality that overrode any lack of vitamin,
felt some unspoken bond with them,

almost like being related, distant
cousins in unconscious Catholicism.

III

Brendan, the most highly-strung & sullen
of them all, a brooder, temperamental,
evinced the vocals in devout tones:
Weller's bark & woof, Foxton's flustered howl,
call & response between blasting guitar
& thundering bass, & the clipped drum-tap
of unflappable Buckler; sharp-suited magpies
pinched in Sta Press, white socks, skinny ties
& black/white bowling shoes pointed sharp
as winklepickers, urchins in funeral suits,
pasty scallywags, hair fringed at the front
unflatteringly, puritanically cropped
from shoulder-length tatterdemalion styles
of the late Seventies—unreconstructed
Mods, the new retro Roundhead breed,
Secondary Modern Diggers, & we dug them!

IV

This was working-class music, common music,
it packed gunpowder punch like saltpetre,
tapped something in us though we felt impostors,
not quite as poverty-carved as pale sculpted
faces on our posters, sons on the shivering
verge, something shivered our spines, shivered
our nerves, something almost regimented
in that aggressive reverb, primitive but tamed,
wild yet disciplined & drilled to rattling drum,
thumping bass & quick-cutting Rickenbacker—
& Weller spat expletives into the spittoon
of his gritted poetry & pockets of pastoral
wistfulness among the glum urban slang
of his language with scapegrace throat-scrapes
of embarrassed sentiment cigarette-singed,
brush of bashful masculinity, boy soldier
brash, fuelled on adrenalin, guttersnipe-
golden of tongue, honeyed hoodlum,

a slug of something strong, nothing on
Aunt Hazel, just silver papers dipped in
flat pints to speed things along, furious
of soul, furious song, & so soul-nourishing.

V

Something in us changed that Sunday once
those sounds sparked us awake, charged us
up with jabbing vibes so we were buzzing
for hours afterwards, our former tastes
for anesthetising synthesisers & synthetic
chic of New Romantics now dismantled
by authentic music of reduced circumstances,
the un-suppressible pulse of up-against-it
optimism, thumping tempo of proletarian
hope—an unreconstructed sound we'd not
forget, which would influence us towards
new tunes & attitudes, socialism of soul,
communism of minds, & help us face up
to tougher feelings when in our future
of domestic scarcity we'd too be sculpted
by poverty, sleep on empty stomachs,
endure sporadic indignities of dole,
forced to sign on & promise to sacrifice
our educations if the job centre found us
work unsuited to our skills & talents—
O we'd soon become bitterly accustomed
to the soul-scouring source of common music.

The Fasters

Is this always to be the sound of home:
the interminable rumbling drone
of empty stomachs—a parent's nightmare:
growing boys' hunger but a larder bare.

The stopped clock governs a timeless room
where ghouls digest morsels in gloom—
Vincent's Potato Eaters recaptured
a century later, on an uncarpeted

hearth, framed in the glow of a cathode ray—
a mute television views our chamber play;
Tausk's Influencing Machine manifest
as a box of frights, a magic-charged cabinet

transmitting images, strange, transgressive,
advertisements of plenty, tempting, intrusive—
a trauma screen like the two-way mirror in
the special clinic mutely reflecting

the absentee son as he sits confessing
horrific thoughts that afflict his schooling—
Hardy's Little Father Time arrested
in clinical forestalling, suspended

in psychical aspic & left to ruminate
on the knotty nature of his tortured state
obscure as their lack, though a boilerplate
label abounded: *the poor are profligate.*

Blow the cobwebs from the crib for Chrimbo,
Christ in a stable, a bloom of fake snow.
As Easter draws near, time to be abstinent:
our fasting at last given symbol by Lent.

Liskeard Eighty-Six

I first found my mind lost in Liskeard
Like the deranged seagulls that encircled it
Even though it was landlocked,
That slaty town of steep narrow streets,
Grey-stoned, interminably bleak—
We'd been taken there on a rickety ride
By obsolete ambulance over beyond
Rain-dark tussocky Cornish hills,
An inaugural Sisyphan pilgrimage,
One of numberless to come, to consult
A Sphinxian psychiatrist to fathom
The cause behind my epic absence
From school, & the pathological
Intrusive thoughts that plagued me,
Made a monster of my mind turning it
Against itself—*Stop trying to be God*
The Delphic psychiatrist said, referring
To my macro-conscience, my sense
Of Olympian responsibility for my family,
For my unhappy parents & the poverty
Of our lives, for everything that happened
To everyone I loved (& everyone I hated),
But I didn't know how else to be, took
My mother as example, her martyrlike
Self-sacrifice for our sakes, her aura
Of Catholic guilt—obsessive-compulsive
Disorder was an obscurer condition
Back in Eighty-Six, probably hadn't been
Properly labelled then but more vaguely
Adumbrated as anxiety or *obsessional
Neurosis*—the psychiatrist, my confessor,
With his penetrating stare, would also
Comment, with an ambiguous smile
& a moral elasticity, that he might
Like a scrapbook of the images
In my mind that tormented me, thought-
Grotesques, attempting to absolve me
Of moral agency so I might readjust

Mentally to the dreamlike (more nightmarish)
Ambiguity of the mind even in daytime,
Stop interrogating my thoughts under
The glare of a moral magnifying glass,
& giving them overimportance,
Omnipotence—but he'd try in vain,
Even though I tried at times to uninvent
My intrusive thoughts, untie the mental
Knot I was in, it never prevailed,
Because instead I ruminated incessantly—
The obsessive's reversion—& each time
I thought I'd 'solved' one thought, I'd find
Several more would grow in its place,
Mutate & divaricate in every direction,
Hadn't yet learned, as I would never,
To burn the stumps of the severed heads
Of this Thought-Hydra to prevent them
Replenishing & growing again
Which was impossibly done by some
Supreme effort of will no one possessed,
Not even a worried god—my mythology
Would go on growing outwards in morbid
Bloom of mouldy Gorgonic carageen
All along the walls of a Byzantine-
Patterned Carrara marble labyrinth
Of deepening imponderables; it would
Be years until I would be diagnosed
But I would come close myself through focused
Reading, ploughing through therapeutic prose
In obsolete self-help pamphlets kept since
The Seventies by a confidence-lacking
Father who'd once tried to teach himself
The rudiments of self-assertiveness as
Advertised in nerve-advertisements—
Nerves was still the vague, almost mystifying
Approximation of my 'problems'—only
A decade or so later would I be prescribed
The chemical means not to burning but
At least numbing the nerve-ends of that Hydra's
Severed heads: serotonin reuptake

Inhibitors; but until then, I remained
Tangled in my homespun mythology
Of worried gods, petrified at the potency
Of thought-power I perceived I possessed,
& all I wished for was to be powerless,
Not a worried god looming over my loved ones,
Surveying every movement & gesture & vibe
& suggestion, just as I sat there feeling
Completely lost in that carpeted room
In the clinic curiously furnished with tatty
Old toys all along its low-lying window-sill,
Discarded infantile comforts, & a sad little
Empty doll's house missing its miniature
Furniture, sparsely decorated with garish
Wallpaper, gazing in on its half-enclosed
Shadowy interiors that made me feel as large
As Gulliver, or giant Alice at the White
Rabbit's house cramped in the creaking rafters
After having drunk from an unlabelled bottle
& grown to enormous size, the pebbles
Thrown in through the tiny windows
Would symbolize my dropsical scruples,
& any little lizard sent down the chimney
Mutate into anything from the fount
Of metonymy just as the strange slaty
& scaly town of Liskeard, its hissing,
Spikey name, like *piskie*, the Cornish for
Pixy, become an aural signature for
The feeling I had at that time, of fright,
Risk & dread, a slowly dawning sense
Of the danger in everything, every thought,
Every feeling, that augured so many
Headstorms to come—a chilly school morning
Sky flaming red, & all I wanted was to feel
Safe & secure, but one cannot escape
From one's own head; maybe I'd not had
Enough discipline instilled in me by my
Liberal upbringing, but the sudden cold drill
Of a martinet school inspector who'd visit me
At home to prod me with his Navy-grey iron

Stare & threaten to have me taken away
To a 'special school' where I'd have to board
During the week, if my school attendance
Didn't improve, was a bitter medicine
Which only traumatised me further, as did
His other threat to prosecute my parents,
& the only way to get a stay of execution
Was to agree to see a psychiatrist
On a twice-weekly basis, & so we did,
For four years, & not once at any point did
That psychiatrist attempt to elucidate
My obscure condition, only ever saying
That I was just *"extremely sensitive"*—
Semantic mystique—or that I suffered
From *"nerves"*, & never revealing to me
The invisible observers on the other side
Of his treatment room's two-way mirror—
I always had the impression that he
Had been more interested in the details
Of those intrusive thoughts & images
& Byzantian ruminations for his own
Private fascination than in trying to find
A way of treating them, but at the time
He seemed to me a friend, the only person
In authority who didn't sit in judgement
Over me, who didn't threaten or criticise
Me, who listened to my deepest anxieties
With no hint on his face of moral shock—
A phlegmatic Sphinx, archetypal self-
Possessed psychiatrist, but the trouble is
He only left me with—to mix metaphors—
The memory of his mystifying smile
Which, like the Cheshire Cat's, eventually
Vanished into vagueness unintrusive...

Bruised Fruit

"I should like the flowers very, very much, if I didn't keep on thinking they'd be all withered in a few days!"

—Little Father Time, *Jude the Obscure* (1890) by Thomas Hardy

I

My parents were lapsed middle class,
They'd skidded down the rungs
Of the social ladder, & came to work
Shifts in manual jobs—Dad's once white
Collar now security blue, mum once
A housewife now a scurrying pink collar
In a care home; we were—as sociologists
Might mythologise it—'relatively
Impoverished', sometimes abjectly,
& were isolated in our privations,
Part of no community, suffering
In partitioned hardship, prisoners
Bound by an unaffordable mortgage
In a dilapidated, unheated cottage.

II

At school—which I intermittently
Attended, more often absent—my
Classmates were working class,
Some were abjectly impoverished,
Indigently thin, etiolated
For lack of vitamin, & I had to pretend
To adapt to their idioms & affectations
Feeling an imposter not in material
Terms but in terms immaterial:
I was of a different sensibility,
A progeny of shabby gentility
& nostalgic residues still yet to be fully

Extinguished, expunged, bruised fruit
Of a chipped China fruit bowl, splinters
Of brittle eggshell-light crockery
Curated by a declassed father
Mentally trapped in the rapt trauma
Of vanished familial comfiture;
Translucent in the unenticing sun
That rinsed me with indiscriminating
Light—a deracinated Oliver
Twist-cum-Little Father Time cast
Into unsympathetic circumstances
Unequipped for the physical sphere,
Left to figure out how to be in a place
Where I had no agency, to find &
Define indefinable fear—fear of losing
Self-identity, petrified of forever
Being defined in the critical macro
Focus of others' consciousnesses,
To be reduced to empty components,
To become complete unperson.

Thus was the curse of classlessness,
Of rootlessness, to be part of no
Community, to share no common
Bonds with other schoolchildren,
To have habits & hopes & interests
& ways of expressing these that were
Out of place among one's classmates,
Never to be accepted as one of their own,
Yet sharing in their immiseration,
Material limitations, reduced
Circumstances—all the while looked
Down upon by those better-heeled
But no more sophisticated in tastes;
To be in limbo between social stations,
Misplaced in purgatorial triage,
Tacitly sent to a Coventry of restive
Nerves & distanced relatives,
My comfort clothes confiscated,
Neither one thing nor the other,

Neither fish nor fowl, but some strange
Amalgam, a chimera of characteristics,
Mixed class, a hybrid, & to feel
Nothing but numbness, emptiness,
Interspersed with fleeting terror,
To regard oneself to be in error,
Faulty, non-functioning, unconnected
To the scenery, insubstantial, an
Aberration, to start at beautiful
Mutations of one's own shadow-aspect,
A thought's desolation, all the beauty
& wonder to be always spoilt by
The prospect of inescapable decay,
Slow bruising shadows—to take no
Joy in fruit for anticipating
Its inevitable bruising & souring
Long, long before its ripening in
The fruit bowl has happened—that is
The nature of my affliction, anxiety,
Dread, apprehension, a praecox
Of trepidation—to not be able to
Enjoy the flowers for seeing them withered
While their petals are still in bloom.

III

Unreconstructed soul,
Out of place, out of time,
An imposter of my species,
Burdened by an incurable
Sense of responsibility
For everything & everybody,
For everything that went wrong,
Weighed down by shadows,
A mind's overcast skies,
& underneath everything,
Every thought, every feeling,
An overwhelming sense
Of dread, of loss, of absence,

Of something fundamentally
Wrong with the world—
No matter how I masked,
No matter how I clowned,
Under it all, the sadness,
Always sadness, washing
Everything in its lachrymose rinse,
Immovable, unfathomable,
The deep & bottomless
Inexpressible sadness
Of existence—the sadness
That is limitless, spaceless,
The stuff of the universe,
The substance of the stars,
The paints of Dutch Vincent...

To only be able to see
The withering in the bloom.

Far Sight

We read the dead, we watch the dead,
We listen to the dead
For our entertainment—
What is the difference between
Sitting round the television
Or conducting a séance?
Both mediums rely on
A modicum of clairvoyance
(& ectoplasmic lubricants)—
What else are radio frequencies
But wavelengths of the grave—
Electricity, a spiritual conductor—
Does the cathode ray tube
Incubate a common soul?

Desolate in Douai

Looking back at our rootless stay in Douai,
The first time I'd been abroad since childhood,
Staying in a mosquito-colonised schoolhouse
Spending our days laboriously trowelling
At an archaeological dig on a rustic site
In a backwater village outside the old town
& its shuttered houses & maisonettes, &
Shady estaminets, exhaustedly excavating
Shards of pottery, subsisting on stale baguettes,
Cheese, & greening salami, barely
Enough francs to scrape for a pack of smokes;
I remember one weekend we took time out
To visit a limited little art gallery, & one
Painting particularly caught my imagination,
Toned in sepia pigments like old daguerreotypes,
Browns, buffs, umbers, beiges, brumal shades—
It depicted three uniformed children
Of the Eighteen Eighties stood together
Petrified to the spot as they looked on
At their portraitist (or stern-faced father?)—
The children looked as if made of China,
Pale faces like porcelain dolls stitched up
In school suits, they seemed somehow separate
From their surroundings, closed-in on themselves,
Locked into their own closeted thoughts,
Shut off to everything not voluntarily but
Pathologically, unreachable, frigid to touch,
Their eyes large & fraught & tortured—I bought
A postcard of this picture & kept it by my
Bedside for the remainder of our days in Douai,
& studied it for hours, something repelled yet
Fascinated me about it, how it was possible,
Horribly possible for some entities to be
Completely separate from their environment,
Completely unconnected to anything around them,
To any person, any other soul, no matter how
Much they might wish to be; & the small
Affectionate French girl Lillie had remarked

Of me that I was so alone, so alone, closed
Off inside myself, unreachable, untouchable,
Unresponsive, & yet I had privately
Coveted her, had wanted to connect with her,
But something was in the way, always, more
Than just shyness or inhibition, extreme
Sensitivity, a haptic handicap, impossibility
Of truly being with another, of bonding,
Of being in love, of being with someone
More than symbolically—but I was like one
Of those painted children of the past, completely
Separate to everything around me, though I
Didn't want to be, was desperate not to be,
But could only express my feelings in fleeting
Poetries, little did I know then, at a mere
Nineteen, when I'd sat on a cold bench in
A French park suddenly frozen by a moment's
Desolation of thought, a sudden realisation
Of how empty & barren & alien the wider
World seemed when cast far away from the warmer
Shores of home, how unfamiliarity felt
Infinitely unknowable & inscrutable,
Infinitely unfriendly, unfathomable,
How distant everything seemed no matter
How close in proximity, & how unadaptable
I was—perhaps if I'd have known then
That I was lost somewhere along a spectrum
It might have helped me navigate the strangeness
Of a world seemingly arranged for anything
& anyone but me, but as it happened, I'd not
Find out this key to making sense of the makeup
Of my masking & sense of no fundamental
Identity until thirty years later—until
That moment of autumnal revelation
That illuminated just as it disoriented me
Moreso than I had already ever been,
I would stay trapped like one of those petrified
Porcelain children in a frame, completely
Of myself, that was no self, completely
Cut off from my fellow beings, completely

Separate from everything—now I understood,
Too, why I'd come out with such enigmatic
Comments casually imparted to others
At that time, that I felt liberated by being
In a foreign country & not knowing its language
For this meant I wasn't obliged to speak,
Didn't feel under pressure to try & keep
Conversations flowing, a selective mute,
But in any case, this experience was only
A much more concentrated picture of how
My very nature was essentially foreign,
Or alien, in any environment, whether
There in France, or in my native England—
Wherever I was I was a stranger, an alien,
Physically present yet mentally absent,
A vaguer version of an idiot savant
Whose own tongue was a foreign language.

Je suis désolé, je suis désolé, je suis désolé.

Berkshire Leaves

With some debt to Tony Harrison's 'The Rhubarbarians'

1.
The leaves are falling in Berkshire now…
Recited my Windsor-born, Datchet-raised father
Wistfully from a hypnopompic poem
Ghost-authored by some Georgian
Composite-poet, Rupert Brooke-cum-Edward
Thomas-cum-Walter de la Mare rolled into
One thoughtform sprung from his nicotined
Tongue as our burgundy Maxi bruised
Into the red-bricked commuter-belt town
Of promised September & self-betterment…

But all I could see ahead were tattered Berkshire leaves,
Flame, auburn, rust-coloured—scraps
Of apocryphal papyrus whirling in the wind,
Tumbling remorselessly as layer after layer
Of my leafy self-esteem flaked away to the rustling
Autumn pavements, yet refused to settle anywhere…

2.
You walk more confidently,
                                        Dad encouraged,
You hold your head up properly,
Your back's straighter, you no longer stoop,
You've better posture, you move more purposefully
Forward since you went there...
                                                Did I? I'd not noticed…
You talk more crisply: I barely recognised
Your voice that first time on the phone;
You've lost your accent & you're catching
Your aitches… You speak more evenly…
You have an air; more sure…
                                        More sure…?
Of what…? Only of how unsure I was,
A Thomas Didymus of no convinced academy,
Arts & angst undergraduate; I might
Have strode more confidently but my heels

Were clueless as to where they were heading;
As for my singed English: three terms' propinquity
To ex-public schoolboys' clipped locutions
Had sharpened up my T's & polished my
Untutored tongue to a fleshy guillotine,
Scourge of lounging vowels, diphthongs brought
Up short, from there on my cutglass
Enunciation would overcompensate
For my comprehensive schooling…

3.
As if by linguistic class-exchange,
One fellow undergraduate, groomed among
The flowing gowns & rose-windowed Gothic
Of Lancing College (that enchanted fortress
We'd see gliding along in the distance from
Our yellow Cortina on the dual carriageway
When I was young) was busy cultivating
Aitch-lapsing, scratching vocal keys across
The beeswax veneer of vintage advantages,
Rhubarbing in verbal rust-brown boxing gloves,
Barking cracked leather jacket vernacular,
A rough diamond cut from R.D. Delderfield's
Wood-panelled dorms & willow-clopping
Playing fields—to swerve them all his days…
I'd not picked up on my pumiced
Pronunciations while speaking on the phone,
Even though my tones echoed round
That rooted red booth begrudgingly grown
From the leaf-heaped rupture of pavement outside
The damp campus: soundproof outpost for
Empty-pocketed scholarships of happenstance
Funded by flagging grants' rag day reversals,
Diminishing returns of barely legal tender,
Croup of loose change coughed up through
Laryngeal clearing; back home, the landline
Had long been cut off at our mortified cottage
Throttled by its albatross-mortgage
(As if things there weren't desolate enough),
So Dad would arrange a day & time in writing

To go out & ring me from a public callbox
On the number of another I'd supplied him;
It was as if we were trying to intercept
Spirit-frequencies, tap ghosts on the wire...

4.
I'd not stood back to appreciate how
I'd shaken off a former stoop & wolfish
Heathcliffian scowl—in truth more the gormless
Glower of the laskar's sickly son, enfeebled
Linton, consumptive valetudinarian;
& I'd once been depicted as a hypochondriac
By teachers, peers & martinet school inspectors
Who couldn't accommodate that I'd been cursed
With enervating "nerves" that sieved my vim
Invisibly for several years, intrusive
Thoughts that stalked me as covert travellers
Only diverted in introspective verses
(Only now, almost forty years later,
Revelated as autism); into these wilderness
Days of rust-red halls, sprawling lawns,
Gloomy dorms & drab pantries painted
Primrose yellow or pale prison blue,
When still a mental truant, a skittish skidder's son
Torn from a civilized tongue to the remoteness
Of a faintly rural twang curling like woodsmoke,
I'd not noticed my metamorphosis from
Chip-shouldered cottage-gnome of no vocation—
Except a poet's impecunious calling—
To upstanding graduate who'd caught the first glints
Of substitute-salvation in vanilla-scented
Ivied quads (pale impostors of Oxford
To which this definitive redbrick university
Was once an annex as its agricultural college),
Spiced with aperitifs of being's bitter absinthe,
Trying to fathom phantasms with out-of-date
Self-help pamphlets scented with cigarettes;
Clumsily attempting to *carpe diem*, brook
Deskbound hedonism, experiencing things
Other than glimpses & figments,

Unreachable pedestals: soul-wringing one-night stands,
Crumpled beds' dead languages, Classics,
Panics, hunger pangs, hangovers & angst…

5.
I routinely bunked lectures to scratch creative itches,
Continuing truant narratives of patchy school days—
Notorious for my prolonged absence-in-residence
At the Classics Department; only my age
Had changed, &, marginally, my range
Of ruminations, but I was still the same,
Still pickled in anxiety's aspic… I rolled slim
Cigarettes from *RIZLA* leaves & dragged-in
Thick afternoons, attempting to pool my
Thumped impulses into foolscap escape-plans,
Amorphous opinions & poems powered on
Dog-ends & blood-coloured tea, rusty as iron
On the tongue; scholarly thoughts scorched
To song-outcrops on paper screes freed from
Clumsily-put metaphors pouring from mouths
Of spruce tutors, Roman fanciers, bookish
Lectors in flannel suits nursing grievances against
Christianity (Scriptures spoilt their appetites
For toga parties; while strictures in indigent guts
Required, ironically, more substantial portions
Of soul food—manna as opposed to canapés);
Sophistication's thorny crown; worshipful tropes
Polishing despots' posthumous reputations,
Gushing round withered laurel wreaths—
No anguishing for Pharisaic popinjays,
Doctoral coxcombs, pedagogic curators
Heaping praise at empurpled hems of temporal
Emperors, groomers of agnosticism
Through rigged assignments to parroting
Insights in tranquilising seminars—

> Q: *How did Peisistratus stamp his legitimacy*
> *As Tyrant of Athens…?* A: *By entering the city*
> *In a golden chariot accompanied by a statuesque*
> *Woman disguised as the goddess Athene—*

Stark contrast to tambourine-bashing Born Again
Christian symposiums, orgies of cardigans
& Tongues-tied glossolalia; or casual
Chauvinisms of textbook Tories—neither
Of these campus cults rubbed off on me,
I was no easy convert to anything other than
What poverty had violently taught me,
Lessons which held more weight, more urgency,
More grit, more authentic, empirical sources
Than second-hand winds of bow-tied ventriloquists
Stringing together glues of borrowed knowledge
At the bottom of snake-pit amphitheatres
Under hundreds of dehydrated student eyes
Thirsting medicines of sifted information
In thin onion-skinned pages like wads of fag papers,
Old Bibles, or psychiatrists' thumb-licked
DSMs—moulted hairs of the dog
For vertigos in pitching lectures…

6.
But there I was, & emptily remained, for three
Purgatorial years attempting to distract my
Rattling thoughts with anaesthetising study,
Stultification of long-filtered after-facts
& antiquated artefacts—autodidact
By nature, conscientious objector
To the bureaucratising of intellect,
Straitjacketing of magical thinking—
My thoughts lost in cognitive rustication;
By the time I'd arrived in those half-hallowed halls,
My remorseless foundation in imponderables
Supplemented with hand-me-down modules,
Ectopic scholarship in penury & neurosis,
Was already completed, had whittled me down
To my core—& all the pomp & trappings,
Ceremonies, cater caps, byzantine rituals, robes
& undisturbed traditions of the academic cult:
Mud that wouldn't stick, water off a mortar board…

7.
I left still a Fresher to self-confidence,
Disorientate, homesick, emptily expectant,
Albeit now a Bachelor of Arts, having scraped
A 'Gentleman's Degree', what W.H. Auden
Gingerly termed the *"Poet's Third"*, replete
With scrolled certificate tied in a bowed ribbon
Inscribed With Honours, though it might as well
Have said *With Sympathy*—all that had rubbed
Off on me was worn in my deportment:
I strode more determinedly, as if expected
Somewhere, spoke more clearly (or brusquely?),
Uncluttered by accent, & had acquired
The art of sustaining eye contact, or making it
Look like I could, & of masking my feelings—
But I'd not noticed these improvements sprung
Up like wishful rumours from my father's mouth
Hoping I'd be spared his stumped options
For having never been to university himself,
A setting in which his scholarly temperament
Would have been much better suited & thrived,
A privilege he'd have grasped more eagerly
Than short straws that grew him into a genteel
Jude Fawley—not only had Christminster spires
Kept their mystical distance from him but also
These humbler chimneys of Hardy's grubbier
Redbridge; so he dug deep into genealogy
To trace ancestors' sepia accomplishments,
& so, vicariously, placate his academic
Inadequacy complex through curatorship
Of our phantom family museum, open to
No public; high scores in IQ tests
& completed cryptic crosswords cut out
From newspapers & left as peeling certificates
Adrift the toilet skirting-board,
Damp parchments of plummeted esteem—
The desperate need to prove his intelligence
To himself, again & again, his joyless hobby...

8.
Back in a bleak slate hamlet, grains of knowledge
Gained from those absent days in a redbrick
Redoubt of brown studies, hadn't smoothed out
My doubts, nor my belated taste
Of Classical education proscribed from state
School syllabus 'bettered' me, as might have been
Expected—my sole motive in having gone
To university had been simply to prove
That I could; all the overripe Ursprache
Pickings of Greek Minor, parched uphill climbs
Through Thucydides, scratchings of Tacitus,
Suetonius, scrapings of Plutarch, Josephus,
Researching, referencing, newly-sprung
Agilities at glossaries, did nothing
To nourish my soul, couldn't stop my stomach
Churning in chilled mornings as frost heaves
Of intrusive thoughts thrust up sharply;
My nerves still hadn't settled yet,
Were still swept along with winds & missed lectures,

like the Berkshire leaves…

Casualties of Verse

Are poets predisposed to accidents, madness,
Suicide & premature death?   *Discuss…*

Christopher Smart, Charles Lamb & John Clare
Were all committed to asylums in states of disrepair;
A fall down the wooden hill knocked big-eyed bohemian
Poet Robert Ferguson into chronic concussion:
Admitted against his will into Darien House asylum,
Next to the city poorhouse, where he died within weeks,
Buried in an unmarked grave in Canongate Kirkyard;
Ivor Gurney slipped up to his middle in a muddle
In Gloucester, then transported to the puddle
Of the City of London Mental Hospital,
Dartford, where his final fifteen years as an inmate
Were taken up with unenlightened treatment
Scarcely bettered since Bedlam, but cold baths
& electric shocks barely registered a prick,
He self-prescribed his poems as purely therapeutic.

Bards without number drowned in their ink.
Both Poe & Monro had problems with drink.
Coleridge prescribed opium as a tonic to relieve
His heeby-jeebies; while his reclusive son Hartley's
Locks shocked neurasthenic white prematurely,
An albino yearling who barely left his stable.
Dylan Thomas milked himself out under a pub table.
Delirium tremens throttled Branwell Brontë.
Scotsman James 'Bysshe Vanolis' Thomson lost sight
Through too many drams of his *City of Dreadful Night*,
Woke with a pounding hangover in dreadfuller daylight…

Depression made Tennyson a Lotus Eater—
One poet even vanished: whither Wendy Oliver…?
The Sussicran-pamphlet *poète maudit* Harry Fainlight
Often hospitalised, who *'lit a petrol-soaked rag'*
& posted it through Faber & Faber's letterbox
In response to their offer to publish him, perished
From hypothermia whilst pneumonic & lying

In a cold dark field wearing only *'light clothing'*—
He'd once defenestrated a typewriter
At his lover Mark Hyatt's flat at 24 Chepstow
Villas, another turbulent bohemian *poète*
Maudit who opted out on a self-prescription
Of sleeping pills & painkillers in April 1972.

Gustaf Froding, Charles Baudelaire, Laura Riding,
Stevie Smith, all attempted suicide with varying
Lack of success—while, passing into myth,
Others succeeded in wiping their shoes on Sisyphus:
Paul Celan, Dino Campana, Thomas Lovell Beddoes;
Chatterton swigged laudanum; Amy Levy choked
Fatally on charcoal fumes—part of a pact
With Olive Schriener, who'd forgotten the contract
Was binding, & had already left the room in fact.
John Davidson took his eternal rest cure off Penzance
Ducking under Cornish water for a cancer he didn't have.

Nicholas Vachel Lindsay, the hobo-troubadour
Of singing poetry, from *Rhymes To Be Traded For*
Bread to *Every Soul A Circus*, slaked his last thirst
By downing a bottle of Lysol: *'I got them first'*—
Got who?
(But his method debuted with Charlotte Mew);
His old flame Sara Teasdale followed only two
Summers after him, found drowned in her bath,
Ophelia topped up on sleeping pills—
All rivers return to the sea; Harold Hart Crane,
Bruised by the knuckles of a male crew member
After his clumsy advances, jumped off
The *Orizaba* with a *"Goodbye everybody!"*
John Berryman leapt from Washington Avenue Bridge
Onto the muddy banks of the Mississippi in
Macabre homage to his self-dispatched father.
Sylvia Plath, Roger Roughton, gassed themselves.
Anne Sexton imbibed lethal fumes with the elves.
Sepuku was the method chosen by the vulnerable
Harry Martinson: scissor snip for besmirched Nobel.

Suicides aside, the accident-proneness of poets
Has, at intervals, depleted their breed: Shelley perished
At sea; Byron sank away with marsh fever while
Campaigning for Greek Independence in Turkey;
The jinxed Rhymers' Club had casualties aplenty:
Ernest Dowson went out with wine but not roses
After his father bought it through tuberculosis,
Which prompted his mother to loop the noose
For fear of reprise; Lionel Johnson, Broadstairs'
Songful son, felled by a stroke after falling from
A barstool; Francis Thompson succumbed to opium
& consumption—lapsed Catholics, all, for want of unction.

Rupert Chawner Brooke died from a mosquito bite;
Dan Andersson was asphyxiated by cyanide
Used to fumigate the bed bugs at Bryggaregatan 5;
Alun Lewis shot himself by accident while shaving—
Or maybe there was something more premeditated
His regiment was camouflaging; obscure, globetrotting
Bernard Spencer was found sprawled by an Austrian railway.
Bluntly, at periods, poets were dropping like tsetse.

Then the Great War's Grand Guignol: mustard gas
& machine-gun whops tore scores of talents
From their lives, or their wits: Wilfred Salter Owen,
Mown down only days before armistice;
Francis Ledwidge, blown to smithereens
While sipping tea in a shell hole; Hedd Wyn
Felled by a nosecap shell; Edward Thomas flung
From willow-clopping Adlestrops to whooping
Flares of Arras' All Out; Flemish mud-flats spared
Few members of diminishing chimers' clubs:
Siegfried Sassoon staggered out of it shell-shocked;
Robert 'Lazarus' Graves, demobbed & posthumous,
Sent home to the snub of his obituary's thumping
Lampblack staves; Ivor Bertie Gurney (again)
Crawled from under barbed wire into the pitching
Night of his soul's Gloucestershire, cradled in
A gurney & transported to a triage station—
But all his hectoring thoughts sought was whistling

Bullets & rumpus of guns to blunt their agitation;
Private David Jones, a war-torn fusilier trudged
Back from the Front's blood-dipped caparison
Pastiche of picnic spreads on rumpling Cal Poly hills
In ancestral Welch Marches his father's lilt instilled
In his soul as a boy in Brockley—now this son returned,
In parenthesis, thought-gored after Mametz Wood.

The Battle for Spain claimed a crop of corduroyed
Poet-communists: Edgell Rickword, John Cornford,
Christopher (St. John Sprigg) Caudwell—but spared
Eric Blair & ambulance-man Auden, pocked
With agitprop of Fascist shot; & the dogged ghost
Of Robert von Ranke Graves (so some consolation
From the ill-equipped Republican Crusade).

The Second World War followed suit: Oxford sparks
To snuffed recruits: Drummond Allison would go
Into *The Yellow Night*, only 22, at Garigliano;
Sidney Arthur Kilworth Keyes captured &
Disposed of just before his 21st birthday
(No doubt serving to appease Philip Larkin's wrath
At his bruising omission from *Eight Oxford Poets*—
The absent ninth!); Keith Castellain Douglas
Hurled by mortar fire to Zem Zem from Alamein…;
Clive Ali Chimmo Branson took a 'glancing' shot
In the back of the head while commanding a tank
In Burma at the Battle of the Admin Box.

Then to Afghanistan & Iraq—who'd count on one
Promising poet among numbers of domino-poppies?
Who knows, or will ever know the uncomfortable nub,
The true human cost of scuppered sand campaigns
Outside the parched prose of lead-pattered scrub?

But to all those poet conscripts who impaled themselves
On the barbs of their age, unwitting fatalities
Of literary enlistment, Artists' Rifles winging off
The written page, we say we will remember them,
And try to find the link from leap to leap, even

If the only point is a stubbed nib—but has there ever
Been a traceable point to the thump of the brain,
The gallop of the heart, the scramble of the pen
In the tumbrel of the hand, the itch to comprehend,
Reflect, describe, emote, that last-ditch attempt
To fumble up the ladder of thought to futile song—
The primal, urgent surge in assembling a poem?

Fox Shadow

Cycling in the night
I saw the silhouette
Of a fox dashing across
The moon-flooded road—
Lean & stealthy,
Ruffled-furred,
Damson-black,
More fox-shadow than fox—
& yet, even in half-light
When a fox is fleetingly visible
With orange fur & white front,
Its feet & legs still look as if
Dipped in soot,
Or in permanent shadow.

Brilliant Blaze

i.m. John Griffith "Jack" London (January 12, 1876–November 22, 1916)

I would rather be ashes than dust!
I would rather that my spark should burn out in a brilliant blaze than it should be stifled by dry-rot.
I would rather be a superb meteor, every atom of me in magnificent glow, than a sleepy and permanent planet.
The function of man is to live, not to exist.
I shall not waste my days in trying to prolong them.
I shall use my time.

—'Jack London Credo', Jack London

Jack was no flash in the pan, his prolific output
Of thirty books in fifteen years paid testament to that,
But his fast life went by in a comparative flash,
Burnt out by forty, collapsed in his prime, partly
From sheer exhaustion, partly from 'accidentally'
Overdosing on morphine he imbibed to soothe
The cramp in his kidneys—by the time his body
Was found heaped in a sleeping porch on his ranch
In 1916 it had endured the ravages of travellers'
Viruses, scurvy, yaws, dysentery, alcoholism,
Uremia... But what a brilliant blaze Jack trailed
Through a furious life, and he could have been a far
Briefer flash had his estranged astrologer father
William Chaney had his way in pressurising
His mother to have an abortion—but Flora
Wellman, of intractable Puritan strain, a music
Teacher and spiritualist who claimed to channel
The spirit of Black Hawk, a Sauk chief, refused
To do so, Chaney then departed washing his
Hands of any responsibility for the unborn child,
The mother shot herself but not fatally & gave
The baby Jack to ex-slave Virginia Prentiss
To look after during her subsequent derangement;
But Flora took Jack back on marrying a traumatised
Veteran of the civil war, John London, whose
Surname Jack assumed—the family then moved
To Oakland, San Francisco... London's biographer

Andrew Sinclair gave his accounts of Jack's life
And work a kick like a brandied aphorism:
'He had a dialectic of appetites without
A synthesis of satisfaction. He once confessed
To wanting to drive forty horses abreast
With the strong arms of his mind…'; by fifteen
Young Jack was already cast in various picaresque
Guises while scrying for his authentic face—gang
Leader, delinquent, sloop-piloting Oyster Pirate,
Klondike tin-sifter, vagrant (for which briefly
Imprisoned)—as he came ashore from the clipper
Sophie Sutherland just as the '93 Panic hit
He determined never again to perform manual
Labour, whether outdoors or in sweatshops,
Never again be *'a wage-slave in the Social Pit'*…

Then the opening of books on library tabletops
For an epic poring—he would complete his solo-
Sponsored sophomoric education entirely by
Himself (though encouraged by poet-librarian
Ina Coolbirth), play both pupil & teacher for
A frantic acquisition of knowledge, a macro-
Scholarship—a San Franciscan autodidact
Acting out his own biopic… Just like his later
Fictional alter ego, the eponymous self-
Educated blue collar-turned-writer Martin Eden,
London became acquainted with the cultured
Middle-class Applegarths whose bookish boughs
Bulged with Swinburne & Browning, but it was
Not only their rarefied lifestyle, tastes & higher
'Altitude' of thought that besotted young London,
It was also the daughter, Mabel, a bourgeois
Marble goddess, &, infatuated, he courted her
Perhaps partly unconsciously as a means to enter
The rapture he felt in hers and her parents'
Presences more permanently, to translate
Into their strata from his less auspicious background,
To jump ships for one-upmanship, to climb
The social ladder—yet, London, a contradiction,
Had a socialistic conscience for his fellow

Working men, yet too was individualistic,
Essentially Nietzschean—no truck with the weak-
Willed or weaklings, even a little fascistic—
Again like Martin Eden who in the end finds his
Self-destruction for lacking faith in his fellow men,
For reading too much Herbert Spencer under
The impression it was impervious wisdom,
Social Darwinism, survival of the fittest,
The *'aristocracy of intellect'*, philosopher kings,
Plato, Aristotle, sweetcorn, barleycorn, amber
Bourbon, damned brandy, Ayn Rand, & all
That sunburnt brain bit—so too had Eden met
His end so suddenly & soon for not listening
To his decadent poet friend Brissenden
That for the conscientious atheist Socialism
Was the only root out from fatalism & self-hate,
Fellowship the cure for death wish, but to Eden
It seemed mere shibboleth, almost as hoary
& weakness-venerating as Christianity,
That old slave religion, manacled morality,
The spiritual aperitif to capitalism's
Main course of labour bondage, wage-slavery...

After Berkeley, Jack packed his trunk for Klondike
To sift for gold, then, on returning to Oakland,
Married Beth Maddern, & more suddenly
& resoundingly than he could ever have predicted,
Broke into the literary world, publishing book
After book in quick succession to swift,
Sometimes stultifying acclaim, &, just as swiftly
Disillusioned with fame, he removed to a newly
Purchased ranch called Glen Ellen... Sinclair said:
'The way out of disgust was love of the people
And escape'—so Jack set sail on a second marriage
To one Charmian Kittredge, then conducted a tour
Of the States lecturing on revolutionary
Socialism, & then to sea, setting off on his
Self-designed ketch, the Snark, to see the world
While keeping up his thousand words a day,
Wrote his most autobiographical novel on

That voyage, *Martin Eden*, only accomplishment
Of that ill-fated trip—Sinclair: *'His mental energy*
Seemed to him at times to be mental sickness';
The ketch nearly bankrupted him: *'Penniless,*
He had to beg an advance from his publisher
To refit the ketch'; London found his checks
Bouncing, the mortgages he had on properties
'Threatened with foreclosure. His teeth, which
Were in terrible shape (unlike Martin Eden's),
Were giving him incessant pain'; and Martin
Eden was a critical and commercial flop, it had
Not been helped by its pessimistic ending &
The suicide of the eponymous protagonist who
Jumps out from a porthole on a passenger ship,
Drowning himself (almost a fictional template
For Hart Crane later)—something London had
Attempted as a youth while the balance of his
Mind was disturbed but he had failed at it…

It's often the way that those most bristling
With life are least afraid of death, even partially
Infatuated with it, & so much of London's
Writing was about *'the struggle of all life*
Against death', Death which he personified as
The *'Noseless One'*, the skull beneath the skin—
An unflinching atheist who stared death straight
In the face; so much of Conrad in London,
So much of 'Lord' Jim in Martin Eden,
'In the destructive element, immerse', so he
Immerses ultimately, wearied by fame,
Wrung-out by overwork to make his literary name,
Haunted by the phrase *'work performed'*,
Tired of performing, tired of life, tired of writing,
And worse, as Eden, *'He has left his own class*
And found it impossible to join a new one'—
Outcast of the strata, neither on land or sea,
Neither fish nor fowl, so he takes his last dip,
His last immersion, his anti-baptism, his
Last swim bubbling Swinburne before sinking…

Eden is destined to alienation not only from
His class & higher circles he swims up to mix in,
But even from his adopted literary vocation
Noting along the way towards eventual
& lightning-sudden success, how strange
& estranging the course of writing is, imagining
'Magazine editors... run a machine that takes in
Manuscripts, puts them through cogs, inserts
A rejection slip, and spits them out'—& that's
Just for those publishers who bother replying;
While working machines in a laundry, Eden
Experiences what it's like to become a human
Machine, an automaton of capitalism's
Production line, wrung dry by *entfremdung*
(How the rough-handed factory flirt Lizzie
Diagnoses of the boho blue collar she fancies:
'Something's wrong with your thinking-machine')—
While Martin's infatuation with the middle-class
'Cultured' Ruth soon dissipates into disillusion
At her genteelly-disguised shallowness
& materialism, & her second-hand grasp
Of academic insights—an intellectual sham;
Sinclair: *"Fancy starch' is the nightmare*
That machines make of Martin's romantic love';
In a fever through overwork of body and mind
'He confuses the laundry and the literary machine,
So that Joe starches manuscripts, while he mangles
The checks in the wringer'—or the rejection slips;
'His ancient typewriter, his Blickensdorfer,
Is a necessity if his writing is to be read
And accepted' (lest we forget Robert Tressell's
Futile attempt to get his hand-written manuscript
Of *The Ragged Trousered Philanthropists* read—
Let alone accepted—by the publishers for want
Of a typewriter) *'when it is pawned, he cannot*
Write'; like Eden, London was a writer
Of craftsmanship rather than inspiration,
Applying himself daily to the toil & trade of writing,
No matter how he felt, no matter the weather,
Even no matter the absence of cigarettes,

He defined himself as a *'blacksmith of literature'*
Forging his furious stories in the prose furnace,
Rather than a *'wordsmith of style and grace'*…

Earle Labour saw in *Martin Eden* London's
Bildungsroman, the story of a young man's
Coming of age, growing into himself, his
Foundation, self-education towards *'a condition
Of dark awareness'*—his version of the previous
Mauve Decade's *Jude the Obscure*; London
Was nothing if not a self-mythologizing writer;
Eden is introduced late into self-consciously
Bohemian circles of Oakland, philosophers,
Writers, based on *'artists and debaters who
Had first met at Coppa's Restaurant in San
Francisco and who formed a colony at Carmel,
Characterised by daily hedonism and occasional
Suicide, abalone-divining and criticism
Of all but themselves'*—a trend of decadence;
But Carmel became Purgatory to London
While the grass seemed greener at Glen Ellen;
*'The myth of individual success through
Hard work still dominated American culture'*
At the time *Martin Eden* was published, so it
Was met with contempt by the Right & the Left:
*'The revolutionary idea that hard work
And success were self-defeating in an unlovely
Mechanical society was unpalatable, both to
Radicals and Republicans'*; & in any case
London's aim of criticising Nietzsche via Spencer
& dissing Social Darwinism by making Martin
A victim of his own individualism backfired
& in fact served to inspire a generation
Of aspiring atheist writers to ruin themselves
With ambition & overwork—Martin being
Seen as a martyr to self-determination
& self-will; & in real life, London was growing
Apart from his supporters who were beginning
To see too much of the rugged individualist
In him, the ketch traveller, the lone rancher,

No discernible behaviours corroborating
The socialism he hypothetically espoused—
Latterly he was seen as an apostate of socialism,
A sell out to his own selfhood, whose truculent
Political convictions appeared to be his potential
Enemy given his fame and wealth: *'As Mark
Twain commented, if Jack London got the kind
Of society he wanted, he would have to call out
The militia to collect his royalties'*; one of his
Ex-comrades wrote to him mockingly evoking
Martin Eden's self-destruction as a possible
Blueprint for him: *'When you swallow the last
Mouthful of salt chuck you can hold before sinking,
Remember that we at least protested'...*

Martin Eden was stormed by the critics for *'it
Denigrated capitalism and self-improvement
And ambition without providing any alternatives'*—
It was *'universally condemned'*; London rescued
His reputation with a return to former more
Optimistic & adventure-oriented fare,
The Klondike-set speculating tale *Burning Daylight*;
But London's disgust with reviewers & even
His readers was only confirmed by the scathing
Reviews *Martin Eden* received—as of his
Eponymous hero his omniscient narrator wrote:
*'His intrinsic beauty and power meant nothing
To the hundreds of thousands who were acclaiming
Him and his books. He was the fad of the hour,
The adventurer who had stormed Parnassus
While the gods nodded. The hundreds of thousands
Read him and acclaimed him with the same brute
Non-understanding with which they had flung
Themselves on Brissenden's 'Ephemera''*,
That stupendous poem of the moment, & *'torn
It to pieces'* after first heaping it with impossible
Praise; *'—a wolf-rabble that fawned on him instead
Of fanging him. Fawn or fang, it was all a matter
Of chance...'*; as Cyril Connolly reminded us
In *Enemies of Promise*: *'Whom the gods wish*

To destroy they first call promising'—itself lifted
From a saying by Menander in the 4th century:
'Whom the gods love dies young'—so for Eden,
So for London, his blaze burnt out at forty;
Yet *Martin Eden* endured, in print ever since,
A failure on first publication but a re-fanned
Flame of influence in the coming *'iconoclasm
Of the 1920s and the anticapitalism
Of the 1930s'*… Sinclair: *'However great his self-
Destructiveness, his mind ranged after the infinite
Possibilities of mankind'*… Yet he courted finity,
To fill up time to the hilt was the highest virtue
To him, he'd *'not waste his days in trying
To prolong them'* but instead use his time to
The utmost, throw thoughts of posterity to
The four winds & let them scatter to ashes,
No dust-heaped tomes in pyramids for him,
He'd rather his *'spark should burn out in
A brilliant blaze than it should be stifled by
Dry-rot… Rather be a superb meteor'*, every
Atom of him *'in magnificent glow, than a sleepy
And permanent planet'*, soul cold as Pluto…

Soft White on Ash Brown

This time it was different: not a cry for help,
You didn't simply scar your forearm, this time
You also took fourteen times the amount
Of Pregabalin, & an accompanying overspill
Of Quetiapine to make a toxic cocktail,
Induce deep sleep which at that moment
You were resolved to be your last, to drift
Off into the soft-pillowed realms of Morpheus,
You just wanted the feeling to stop, the feeling
Of unquenchable anger, unappeasable pain,
& gut-wrenching guilt at having felt
You'd caused me emotional suffering—
At that moment you'd chosen to let yourself slip
Into deep endless sleep in order to spare me
From the second hand pain caused by the ever-fresh
Flaming pink scars of your first hand agonies,
Like burns, like urticaria—nettle-rash,
That is—& your nerves are nettled, constantly
Prickling across your paper-thin skin;
Thank God you came through, woke from that sleep,
It was touch & go, but isn't every breath
& heartbeat; I made sure to rouse you
As early as possible to make sure you
Were okay (if that's not an inadequate word),
& brought you round with a cup of sugary coffee,
Lovingly made, a pale brown soup or potion,
Milky like the misty light dissolving
In your dark hickory eyes, like the soft white
Sun chalked across your ash brown hair.

The Four Spoons of Phineus

Spoon One: *Phineus Among the Harpies*

The appeal was refused by the tribunal, the tribunal
numbered three: an insouciant judge, a glacial lawyer,
& a GP who wilfully misinterpreted him,
pinned him at cross-purposes, kept making a point
of his insight & articulacy—qualities going against
his case, as if to imply the mentally afflicted must be
stupid, when it's almost always the opposite case,
her assumption that intelligence bestows prolific
phrenic equipment to cope with any symptom of mind,
even the *ego-dystonic* (a term he'd picked up from
some foxed blue-spined Pelican—pain makes its own
experts~~—pure aphorism~~), attempting to explain
the impetus of Pure Obsessional Disorder:
that it matters not one whit whether he would act
on his intrusive thoughts, present risk, this bore
no relevance to the intensity of distress ~~felt~~,
the inexorable anxiety rooted in uncertainty,
mutating symptomatology ~~(disclaimer: more ugly
jargon again)~~, a mind besieged by obsessions
~~(tautology: the Latin root obsessus means besieged)~~;
something about him caused them umbrage,
the three 'impartial' panel members, apparently
'independent' from Independent Assessment Services
(Atos formerly), & the Department for Work & Pensions;
pernickety Harpies handpicked for nitpicking
pedantry pecking at the scraps of his incapacity—
he, a hapless Phineus, half-crippled by phobias;
supposed experts deciding his entitlement, or not,
to Personal Independence Payment (PIP ~~(excuse
the parentheses)~~); they even used his avoidance
behaviours against him to argue that he was high-
functioning in spite of therapists' emphases
that these repetitious rituals are not coping mechanisms
but symptoms that retard healing of psychical scars;
he might have quoted Kierkegaard, something along

the lines that all the torments of the damned pale in
comparison to anxiety: excoriating guilt
of the innocent, gut-aching angst* from the Latin: *angere*: to choke
in the absence of an act ~~(Hamletic hesitation)~~,
spent nerves of no event, but that would have also
gone against him—as did his having been to
university, &, more intrusively, that creative
writing was his 'hobby' ~~(how suburban that sounded!)~~
which makes him probably a bit bohemian,
thus unreliable, rebellious, anti-establishment,
& while he might convince as an idiot savant,
he'd obviously been embroidering the truth to a more
threadbare brocade when claiming he was number-blind,
they pointed out he'd have had to tackle statistics
while studying Sociology~~—not as far as he~~
~~could recall, but in any case he'd later changed~~
~~to Ancient History~~... At school it took until he
was fourteen to see what the clock face had so long
been screaming at him, a lightning-struck Damascene
of horology! Now Old Chronos could no longer
cock a snook—a little death erupted in him then,
a peripheral epiphany, still trapped in fight or
flight of tick-tock neuroticism permanently
ruminating on past & future, never mentally
in the present, temporally absent, but at last able
to tell the time without having to guess it, now
everything pressed more urgently, reassurance
in grasping butterfingered suffering was as
time-limited as contribution-based benefits...

Spoon Two: *Phineus Suspected of Parasitism*

The appeal panel was meant to be independent,
yet the scent of preconceived opinion
as to Phineus's suspected parasitism
overwhelmed the impersonal chamber, a courtroom
facilitated to scrutinise the incapacitated
(presumed guilty of malingering until proven
otherwise), impeach the poor, unemployed,
unemployable (though it had nothing on
the courtroom of his own accusatory thoughts
that never show him mercy & always arrive
at the most vindictive verdicts), consciously
misconstruing honest accounts & taking
offence at courtesy, as if attempted flattery,
choosing to perceive evasive evil in the most
ingenuous of gestures, an impertinence
imperceptible because it simply isn't there at all,
imagined sleights—as if being observed by
Victor Hugo's pathologically conformist
Inspector Javert whose morally forensic eye
sees evil everywhere, who abhors rebelliousness
& the bohemianism from which he himself
sprang (son of a gypsy fortune-teller), scourge
of escaped convict Valjean[* *Les Misérables* (1862)],
or Herman Melville's faintly satanic Master-at-
Arms Claggart, arch-antagonist to Billy Budd,
the young Adonic sailor & foretopman whose
innocence & uncorrupted beauty he simply
cannot countenance[** *Billy Budd* (1891/1924)];
a courtroom for scouring out the sick & unlucky
with pedantic pumice stones of *'I put it to you'-s*,
rough pebbles of scruples[***] cross-questioning
the unfit as if criminal suspects simply for
making claims of the State that makes examples
of them in pop-up judgement theatres,
treats them as if their afflictions are their fault,
behavioural foibles, *'lifestyle choices'*...

& so the appeal was refused~~, as Phineus felt~~
~~in his bones it would be~~—in spite of all the facts—
as he rose from the chair ~~(*without using its arms*~~
~~*for support* as it was noted)~~, staggering towards
the savage daylight of Havant gazing in against
the glass from outside the suitably Brutalist
tribunal building like an outraged vigilante
raging at a convicted child molester being
bundled into a van with a blanket over his face
~~that might as well be an inverted spit hood~~
(the kind of graphic imagery suggested in his
agitated head)—then there was a hailstorm,
traumatic, that clattered at the windows &
drummed on the grass verges as the darkening
sky bruised Navy blue & thundered, then halted
abruptly as it had started, like a panic attack,
sun blazed back, his mind pounded, thoughts
left tattered, melted for scrap ~~(is this lapsing~~
~~into rap?)~~ as he wound his way back across
the rough concrete rail bridge that combed the shabby
precinct with half its shops shuttered & graffitied...

They'd evidently decided he was a wolf-
crying chronic hypochondriac ~~(metaphorically~~
~~lycanthropic perhaps?)~~, a maladaptive
specimen of Munchausen's syndrome by proxy,
or some such psychosomatic ailment,
what used to be more evocatively termed
valetudinarian (back at school he'd always
haunted the sickbay), anything but actually
what he was: one of countless psychical casualties
of elliptical descriptors, psychological
refugees snagged on Kafkaesque paper
spikes, cast on a scrapheap, cash-strapped,
ripe pickings for Harpies as he had been
as a boy absentee ~~(please excuse the ellipses)~~...

[Note *** etymological tautology: scruples is from Latin *scrupus* meaning 'rough pebble', which also figuratively means anxiety]

Spoon Three: *Phineus & the Eighty-Eight Statements*

Phineus wrote to the Tribunal requesting
a Statement of Reasons for their refusal
of his appeal with view to appeal to the Upper
Tier Tribunal, the document made plainer
their pejorative view of his character—
he'd not even been aware it was his character
they were scrutinising but simply his claim
to the benefit & the validity of it—& that they
detected 'a pattern' ~~(how apt since he always~~
~~saw patterns in everything—especially~~
~~on spectrums)~~ in the timing of his appointments
to re-up-take therapy, apparently sometimes
merely days after some negative benefits
decision, as if to impute his symptoms
were only prompted whenever the Department
for Work & Pensions intercepted him
periodically & seemingly to little purpose
but simply to disrupt & upset his temporary
respite from financial worries, the precipice
to which all claimants are intermittently
pushed by the repeat-offender of the State
~~(their invisibly abusive partner, or parent)—~~
& that's not simple paranoia, but empirical
paranoia, those tan paper envelopes provoke
catastrophic thinking in panicked recipients...

The document that detailed the justifications
for their negative decision spanned thirteen
pages & eighty-eight individual statements—
as brutalising as that initial traumatic
assessment—giving reasons as to why
they'd gazed on him unfavourably—& what
a revelation, these eighty-eight statements!
It seemed these three Seers had peered deep
into Phineus's soul & understood
the aetiology of his ego, his deepest motives,
& now set about telling him so many things—
~~eighty-eight in all!~~—about himself, his true

nature, the measure of his symptoms
& condition, things he'd have otherwise
been cheated of knowing had he not by
some strange & self-flagellating urge
written to request their Statement of Reasons,
their omniscient witness to his character,
nature & mental constitution, their Olympian
probing of the cloudy pool of his soul—
indisputable Eighty-Eight Statements
that have started a whole new chapter in
the byzantine narrative of his moral character,
~~his evidently deviant drive, manipulative mind,~~
these Three Seers had divined his true
intentions to deceive in order to receive,
they conveniently framed his entire claim
in this narrative of acquisitive behaviours
& innate sense of entitlement to state handouts—
~~so is he~~ accused implicitly of being a scrounger,
sponger, idler, malingerer, a workshy layabout,
a parasite of incapacity—of course, in truth
he is none of these, not a spinner of suspiciously
unprescribed complaints, no symptom-impostor,
not slothful but fatigued, Phineus is a spoonie*
with only four spoons left; yet what of all
the documented evidence, decades of medical
& psychiatric correspondence, prolific paper
trail of prescriptions: Xeroxat, Fluoxetine,
Sertraline—presently Phineus was taking
Mirtazapine, which helped him sleep whilst
stimulating his appetite, ~~the means to which~~
~~he started eating solids again after a long~~
~~bout of soup-sipping depression, trapped~~
~~in fight or flight, stomach constantly churning~~;
nevertheless, the Eighty-Eight Statements
made a point of picking apart his points
piece by piece mean-spiritedly, scraps for
the Harpies, no he wasn't sporadically
self-employed, it was periodic *'permitted*
work/ therapeutic earnings' ~~(O Sisyphean~~
~~scrape of existence in unemployment's open~~

~~prison)~~ still they pointed out apparent
contradictions in his points, punctuated
themselves with perverse interpolations,
tortuous interlocutions, ~~serpentine
imputations,~~ these Harpies depicted Phineus
as Sphinx, seeing the cryptic in nuances—
their Eighty-Eight Statements were classic casuistry,
their Eighty-Eight Statements were processed sophistry,
their Eighty-Eight Statements were pure ~~prose~~ poetry...

[Note * A spoonie is someone living with a chronic illness. It mostly refers to physical chronic illnesses, though it has been known to be a helpful term for those with chronic mental illness as well. It originates from Christine Miserandino's Spoon Theory story, in which she explains what it's like to live with chronic illness to a friend, & uses a handful of spoons to demonstrate (Urban Dictionary)]

Spoon Four: *Phineus Refused Permission*

Now to the latest episode in this piteous soap
of foolscap and brown paper envelope: Phineus
heard back from the Tribunal after responding
to the now almost mythical Statement of Reasons
~~& its many mythologems~~ with an even denser
document detailing his many arguments, points
& claims of *'errors of law'* in the tribunal's
decision to refuse his first-tier appeal, & had his
request for permission to appeal to the Upper
Tribunal refused because they did not agree
with him that there had been any 'errors of law'
but that all had been decided in accordance
with the 'facts' as they were seen by the Harpies
of Appeal pecking away at the carapace &
plastron of his case as if out of some strange
judicial spite & perplexing, poorly disguised bias
towards the DWP & Atos assessor as sacrosanct
oracles, unquestionable & beyond reproach
in spite of prolific reports pointing out their ~~corrupt~~

warped protocols & institutionalised sleight-of-hand,
prompting Phineus to call them out: *just how is*
this Tribunal 'independent' or impartial? as well as
requesting ~~by Freedom of Information~~ the precise
occupational titles of the two ~~so-called~~ *'professionals'*
~~(are Harpies *'professionals'?*)~~ be disclosed as
he suspected neither of them had the faintest
clue as to the symptoms, nature & dynamics
of his particular affliction & how it affects him
on a daily basis in terms of meeting the slippery
descriptors with their pointy spikes like seaweed-
slimed rockpools designed to stub the toes & blunt
the mind, split the will & cripple the spirit while
all the time the cliffs of officialdom either side
constantly shifted & threatened to crunch together
& crush the appellant in-between their barnacled
grind, Symplegades of the Department for Wreckers
& Pirates who have long garnered infamy for
running so many sea-going Argonauts of indigence
~~—rag Argonauts—~~aground, shipwrecked & left
for vultures, Valkyries &, not forgetting, Harpies
to pick at their scraps & make sport of their pain
& anguish amid the carrageen-clung ruins
& tooth-stump Doric columns of past temples
where Phineus attempts repast only to find all
that's left of his rotting fruit after the Harpies
have had their picks are the peels barely edible
& bitter on the palette but the best he can hope
for apart from tins, but he has no can-opener,
so has to bash them against bits of rubble
to put a dent in them then sip through a slit
the juices within, cut his tongue on the sharp
jagged metal as he imbibes mandarin brine
mingled with haemoglobin, O replenishing
non-perishables to his slurping epicurean,
such rusty metallic-tasting fare, unappetising
pulp of processed hope, reconstituted nutrients
& vitamins with e-numbers & additives,
addiction-giving sugars, skimmed Ambrosia,
tinned *Carnation* for lotus-eaters, artificial mush,

slimy, greasy Soylent Green for claimant ruminators,
blinded by the hot prongs of bureaucratic protocols;
scrimping Phineus has always thought at bottom
he's an idol of idleness, a living advertisement
for invisible invalidity (misinterpreted as lazy
due to his delayed sleep-phase disorder
which means mornings are a scourge for him,
though un-diagnosed~~—in fact, most GPs haven't
heard of it yet~~—along with likely high-functioning
autism/Asperger's: probable Phineus is somewhere
on the spectrum), a thorny-crowned toga-ragged
Effigy of Scrounging, a Paragon of Sponging…
All this implicit & imputed by those appeal
panel Harpies' unsympathetic verdict & refusal
to grant him permission to appeal to the Upper
Tribunal, the one scrap granted him now in his
tortuous odyssey towards distant misty topsails
of the ship of PIP, the possibility of applying for
an oral hearing of his request for permission to
appeal to the Upper Tribunal in spite of having
already had permission refused, to apply for
permission to request permission again for
the opportunity to put his case to the Upper
Tribunal, simply fill in the form, the soul-scouring
form, but be prepared permission to request
permission in spite of refused permission may
still be refused, ultimately, or penultimately,
as the case may be… Some of their points were
mistaken, a mere slip of the pen, not errors
on points of law, ~~just slips of pen-points—~~
even if the documents were typed, implicitly,
computer-processed, Phineus's colophon,
Phineus is a slip of the pen, ~~a slip of a person,~~
an incapacitated myth, a claimant Icarus,
a liver-pecked Prometheus, a crippled Bellerophon,
& so is his Pegasus, its wings limp & broken, still
yet he waits patiently, perpetually, for permission…

Phineus' Pyrrhic Triumph: Four Spoons Spent!

There was no trumpet fanfare to announce his triumph,
it was a small stumpy triumph, but a triumph none-
the-less of principle & true endurance over
bureaucratic spite & expedience, after all
the trauma that the Department for Whiphands
& Punishments had put him through, all those
hoops & spoons, smoke & mirrors without moral
compasses he'd had to navigate, Byzantian
rabbit holes of claim forms, traumatic assessments
that exacerbated symptoms swept aside,
mandatory reconsiderations, caucus races,
tribunal hearings & being deliberately misinterpreted,
misunderstood & accused of being some kind
of sickness-collector, an indigence-addicted
malingerer, certainly the Tribunal had taken
the ~~dim~~ view that he was obviously, ~~definitively~~
valetudinarian simply due to his voiced observations
of various conditions ascribed to him, ~~prescribed him,~~
he lost many points for having *'insight'* into his
ailments, for being demonstrably able to articulate
prolific symptoms & to form opinions on them,
in short, he was not an evident mental defective
as they seemed to unreconstructedly characterise
those who suffer mentally ~~(what ableism!)~~, as if it's
somehow an intellectual failing, a form of idiocy,
as if Phineus should, according to his conditions,
be a simpleton or at least have the decency
to feign authenticity as an elective mute or
idiot savant—that was just about the verdict
of those Harpies of Appeal at Havant; & he always
used to joke whenever he passed that place on the train
"I haven't been to Havant" but now he can say
"I definitively have been" & all he saw of it was
a windswept precinct with half its shops shuttered,
a concrete station bridge & a Brutalist assessment
centre whose entrance was more like an airport
clearance with black-clad security guard scanning
his bag & beeping him in--& a vast waiting area

empty as a departure lounge after take-off, where
he sat in echoey desolation awaiting his tribunal...
That Tribunal postponed Phineus's entitlement
to PIP on spurious pretexts, by another year, &
although he eventually managed ~~by mandatory~~
~~reconsideration~~ to overturn the original decision
& be granted basic daily living component there
will never be any compensation for those two
punishing years during which he battled for
entitlements speciously denied him ~~time & again~~
as if he'd been imagining his agonies of mind;
so Phineus triumphed in the end although he
tends to think of it as a Pyrrhic victory
because his conditions are chronic, chronic as
his impecuniousness—one of tens of thousands
of spoonies scooped off the DWP production line
in spite of its purported purposes—& will
only worsen & come to a point when simply
having a few extra points & pennies makes
precious little difference as time & contributions
ebb the way of all earthly benefits ~~& runcible spoons~~...

Demosthenes at the Pharmacy

Waiting for my prescriptions I overheard
Another customer being asked for his
Surname & he said: *DEM-OS-THE-NES—*
That's D-E-M-O-S, DEMOS, THE, and
N-E-S—That's Greek isn't it? I asked,
Once a Classics graduate (but that's all
Ancient history now); *Yes, Greek Cypriot*,
He answered; *Demosthenes*, I verbally
Ruminated, then remembered: *Ah yes,*
Of course, Demosthenes, he used to
Gargle with pebbles to overcome his
Stutter for public oratory—Yes, said
Mr Demosthenes, *I've heard a lot of odd*
Stories about him, then, we were both
Stumped as an awkward silence fell,
Since a packed pharmacy was hardly
The place to discuss ancient Athenian
Statesmen like Demosthenes who, as well
As speaking with pebbles in his mouth
To help overcome his speech impediment,
Was said to recite verse while running,
& send his stentorian voice from the shore
Thrown over the waves' leonine roar—
As in Ancient Athens, so in modern Bognor.

Marzipan / Mirtazapine

I take my marzipan at night
I have to because it makes me sleepy
If I ate it during the day I wouldn't
Be able to stay awake much less
Operate any machinery
(Not that I operate machinery)—
I suppose this makes me a spoonie...

The marzipan makes me sleepy,
It soothes me, wraps itself around
My tired mind with its sweet enveloping
Softness slowly yellowing to sepia
Thoughts & a warm vagueness
Something like a gold nostalgia glow,
An analgesic religiousness,
A hypnogogic halo-glow—-
Envelops my Battenberg mind...

Marzipan has properties plentiful
To appease depressions,
Dampen anxieties, let peace seep in
To the emptying mind, spread
Sweet as frangipane, sweetly thickly...

But one of the side effects of marzipan
Is it stimulates my appetite,
Stimulates my appetite,
& it's better not to eat at night,
Because then you can't burn off the fat,
So it simply accumulates, heaps itself
Around the hips & waist
Like jabbing hands, gripping phalanges...

Marzipan sweetens bitter almonds
Of the brain, bitter almonds of the brain,
Something of a paradox because
Marzipan is made from almonds,
Marzipan & almonds are one & the same
Just as sad & happy, mad & sane,
How one takes them depends on taste…

So next time you take your marzipan
Bear in mind it's a kind of immunization,
& that there are some ramifications:
Mirtazapine is no mere Diazepam...

Dendrochronology

My father's brown wooden hands,
Fingers like gnarled twigs,
The ink-blue veins bulging like wires
Through the skin revealing the aged workings
Of his physiology—the bark is
Being abraded, layer by layer,
Mottled with spots, marks & blotches,
& ever more alarming moles—
Melanomas?—yellow, tan, brown,
Black constellations of dark stars against
Pale carnation backdrop of epidermis;
& rings everywhere, girdling the fingers,
Bagging the eyes—dendrochronology
Of dotage on this gnarled, twisted,
Brittle eighty-three year old tree—
There's no longer gentleness in rough old age,
Not enough time for nuance or subtlety—
Now, when I look in the mirror, he says,
I no longer recognise my own body.

Young Wystan

The Thirties was a period of poetic preponderance
On the burgeoning weight of a Guilty Generation
& its slippery grasp of an approaching apocalypse
Of moral composure, a scorched catastrophe
At the fag-end of ashtray hiatus, a Moment
When Poetry & Politics, Art & Action,
Would converge, become symbiotically one—
Such hopeful projections gushed donnishly
From the graduate pen of one Wystan Hugh
(W.H.) Auden whose vaguely Nordic-sounding
Surname beckoned Icelandic ancestors cut
From basalt crags of black Gabbroic sagas
& volcanic ash in his fanciful imagination—
Though its etymology was more probably Anglo-
Saxon, from Ealdwine, meaning *'Old Friend'*,
Or Alden, meaning *'Half-Danish'*, while his own
Generational roots were in Birmingham,
A city singed into a vastly contrasting Black Country;
In the mid-Thirties, he penned to his old prep-
Friend, Christopher Isherwood, a polemical
Birthday poem in which he augmented his
Private anguishing in the *'squalid shadow*
Of academy and garden' as to some guiding
Light to ignite their beleaguered generation,
To *'Make action urgent and its nature clear'*;
& here the young Oxford-finished smoky hope
Of Rookhope (his *'sacred landscape'*) would see
His name leased out to a mystical meta-terrain,
Which he termed a *'fabulous country'*—a truly
Fabular landscape where unicorns would not be
Out of place—which came to be commonly
Canonised *'Auden Country'*: actually more a county,
But a parabolic county of sunny uplands sprawled
Somewhere between the flat Midlands & crinkled
Home Counties, or further-flung Durham, or,
Figuratively, *'Between the idea/ And the reality/*
Between the motion/ And the act', where falls
The etiolated shadow—Eliotian night—

Of hollower realms shocked with reticent corn
Of moral doubt, scorched conscience, indecision,
Hamletic hesitation, & self-prickling cacti
Of 'Sin'-preceding angst, Skaldic bleakness bespeckling;
A metaphorical place, a figurative territory
Without frontiers or turrets between literature
& action, a quilted inertia, one rinsed
Of Cartesian cadastrals scattered like patchworks
Across partitioned pastures warped by one-
Upmanship, class distinctions, neuroticism,
Grimacing scarecrows, leafless winter hedgerows
Cauterising essential seams that once stitched
Together old gnarled bedfellows of private
Art & public action; sprouted lustrous trees
Of self-expression branching rich scrolling
Foliage of Socialism, filigrees of fellowship—
Where now are only knuckled stumps,
Stubble fields, overcast skies, bite of rosehip,
& a simmering fascism of the shires...

From the outset of his self-transcending bardic
Dialectic, his distinct, self-influenced 'Audenic'
Discipline, the brilliant boy from Solihull,
Embryonic Brummagem Bard, third of three sons
Born in York to physician Charles Augustus,
& the picturesquely named Constance Rosalie
Bicknell, missionary nurse, Young Wystan—
Graced with the cloistered face of a scholarly
Twelfth-century friar, carved eyes bevelled
With the belfry-dark of meticulous craft
On parchment & illuminated manuscript,
Skin freckled like bookish foxing—sent out
Mixed signals, sparring shadows always latticing
His path: first he was for defining an authentic
Political poetry—then, for obfuscating
Such lofty tolls for the subtler peals of *'parable-
Art'* (but surely all Art was parable?); in his
Introduction to *The Poet's Tongue* (1935),
Auden coined this Grail again as *'The parabolic
Approach'*, the quintessence of which was Poetry;

This Parabolic Poetry would teach us *'Love'*
But not *'ideology'*, would bear us messages
In paradigms, the sides, ours to decide—rather
Than being didactic, it would lead us out from
Dingy dorms & gloomy schoolrooms of ethical
Tutelage, moral rhetoric, out to ecchoing
Greens of chainless heart-intelligence, or up
To flights of self-enfranchisement through
Hermeneutic Choice, personal responsibility
For interpreting the parable with whichever
Messages seemed to strike us first in the figurative
Tapestry—& this was where Anxiety entered,
Gingerly, with its weighted gingery grin:
Neurosis, a residue sourced from a species'
Rinsing sin, the *'dizziness of freedom'*, Chagrin
Of Choice, the choking chain of impossible
Office, or whichever Kierkegaardian
Coinage one picked, Anxiety was the defining
Temperament of the time—in tandem with
Ennui—not only for the Audenites, but also
Their initialled progenitors: Nottingham's
Flame-haired David Herbert (D.H.) Lawrence,
& cat-like trans-Atlantic catch, Thomas
Sternes (T.S.) Eliot who had once admitted
To himself that *"Anxiety is the hand maiden*
Of creativity"—thunderstruck lightning-
Charge of Damascene anticipation;
Auden would augment his moment to neurotic
Crescendo with *The Age of Anxiety:*
A Baroque Eclogue in Anglo-Saxon consonance,
His definitive break from formative verses,
First twist in the path away from Young Wystan
Through blue smoke & murky cocktails
To chunky onyx ashtrays & wrinkled skin
—A pickled walnut in Manhattan...

Walnut Manhattan

By 1939 Wystan Hugh Auden's poetry
Was becoming almost criticproof, tobacco-
Gin-&-vermouth-soaked, thick as his puckered
Walnut-shell skin, & his much-lauded name,
Lauded Auden, cod-Icelandic clothbound brand:
His impermeable reputation had been
Pre-stamped with posterity (few poets
Experienced such apotheosis while still alive)
& consolidated in a 1937 *New Verse*
Published in tribute to his dog-eared genius,
Contributors numbering Louis MacNiece,
Edgell Rickword, & one young green pseudo-
Surrealist called Dylan (pron. Dullan)
Thomas who said of the Birmingham-made
Marbleised effigy in his lofty thirtieth year:
'I sometimes think of his poetry as a great war,
Admire intensely the mature, religious,
& logical fighter, & deprecate the boy
Bushranger', then spiked his tribute with
A sardonic aftertaste: *'P.S.—Congratulations*
On Auden's seventieth birthday': so historied
As the name 'Auden' already sounded,
Particularly to those up-thrusting New
Apocalyptic poet-striplings whose talents
Had barely ripened under the Odinic
Gaze of the Brummie Master, that 'Aulden'-
Sounding name that sounded as if it had
Always been there insinuated in the aural
Atmosphere, long before the old soul
Was born to occupy its scooped-out casing,
& so it was not such an audacious leap
To anticipate he'd already reached
His three scores & ten, if not in actual figures,
Then figuratively speaking; not all tributes
Were without criticism (apotheosised
Poets have apostles but also apostates):
George Barker's contribution was to discern
In the verse of the pedagogic Brummagem Bard

'A clumsy interrogatory finger questioning
Me about my matriculation certificate,
My antecedents, & my annual income'—
With such boisterous & bolshy, crooked-tied
Schoolboy recalcitrance, Barker furthered
That he also sensed '…*a sort of general*
Conspiratorial wink being made behind
My back to a young man who sometimes
Has the name Christopher, sometimes Stephen,
Sometimes Derek, & sometimes 'Wystan'',
Expressing his dislike of this detectable
'Snobbery of clique'—but providing the rear-
Guard to Auden's Quadrangle-Hydra of talents,
The only name not cited by Barker, 'Cecil',
Paid tribute to his peer & mentor: '…*No*
Contemporary writing shows so clearly
The revulsion of the artist from a society
Which can no longer support him, his need
To identify himself with a class that can
Provide for his imagination…'—cue the oak-
Panelled Oxford Communism percolated
At a corner of Peckwater Quad where Sage
Auden held court; while equally well-
Educated Edgell Rickword couldn't resist
Taking a chip at the eponymous benefactor
Of so much Audenic hagiography, writing
Of his poetry, in an essay, 'Auden & Politics'—
The subject & title, backhanded compliments:
'…*the feeling of insecurity that afflicts*
A section of the middle classes as the ceaseless
Concentration of capital into fewer hands
Undermines their comparatively privileged
Position'—one which Rickword also occupied;
Skelton, in retrospect, noted an earthier,
Chthonic tonic key in Auden's oeuvre:
'Some poems, at once explicitly sociological
& deeply personal, invoke nature as a restorer,
Not of repose, but of strength & fecundity'—
& here were the seeds of Lawrentian vitality
Sown deep in the long-ploughed furrows

Of Auden's painstakingly cracked face...
John Fuller's dedication to Auden's oeuvre
Was thickly bound three decades later:
A Reader's Guide to W.H. Auden (Thames
& Hudson)—a compendious companion
To the thirty-odd titles up to 1970,
Comprising twenty volumes of verse, three plays,
Three film scripts, four librettos & three
Musical accompaniments, one a song-cycle,
Obsessively catalogued & criticised,
Warts & all appraised—Fuller wasn't shy
Of picking up on Auden's less lauded flaws
& contradictions (all expressed in present
Tense since the subject was still existent
& contemporaneous when it was written,
Though, as with the poor—& the rich—Auden
Is always with us, is somehow immanent
As the timelessness of his 'Icelandic' name):
'Auden is frighteningly at ease with ideas,
& likes occasionally to both tease & hector
His readers. He is not often emotionally
Demonstrative in his poetry, & is one of
The most challengingly adroit versifiers
There has ever been'—Auden was as self-
Possessed as his landscape-shaping name,
Auden was simply Auden, authentic article
Of his own manufacture, begat of himself:
'He has been his own kind of Lawrentian,
His own kind of Marxist & his own kind
Of Anglican'—almost an afterglow to his
Guru & publisher at Faber & Faber,
The mystically initialled supreme template,
T.S. Eliot, poet-archimandrite,
His own kind of Carlist & his own kind
Of Anglo-Catholic—both poets, too,
Were enshrined as 'Anglo-Americans':
Eliot for having emigrated to England
From America, & Auden for having done
The reverse (naturalised across the Pond
To be with Chester Kallman, his golden-haired

Apprentice, cohabiting platonically
In a sprawling apartment where blue smoke
Curled up past white wood panelling
Behind a façade of Brooklyn brownstone—
Later, they flighted & alighted in Austria)—
Both initialled poet Titans were the poem-
Supermen of their respective generations;
Eliot, more drawn to the Teutonic, Siegfried,
& German Volk; Auden, to obscure Nordic roots,
The Scandinavian traditions, the Dread
Of the Danish, Kierkegaardian angst towards
His *Age of Anxiety* in the Forties, all marking
'His progress from Saga to High Table',
Tongue bound to Yggdrasil, eyes upwardly
Gazing to the vaults of Valhalla from
A draughty station platform waiting room
In the Home Counties, doilies, whistling kettles,
Valkyries of shaking China kaolinite,
& nicotined teapots…)—Auden was, it seemed,
A creature of phases, an amorphous shape-
Shifter, never wholly committed to any
Of his donned prosopons of the moment,
Yet each sported a patina apparently
Authentic on closer inspection, signatured
With craftsmanly verisimilitude of fake
Antiques—1933 was, to Fuller's mind,
Auden's *'great year for discarded neo-*
Marxist work, a year in which Lawrence seems
To have been put behind him, & a year…
Of some artistic turmoil & choice of direction,
One might well have expected a more decisive
Move towards a religious position' (viz.
Eliot)—& for the remainder of the Thirties:
'Auden's energies in the following half-dozen
Years were to a great degree technical:
In ideas he stood fairly still. … We know it
Now to have been only a phase, just as
The early oblique poetry of disappointed love…
& the middle Rilkean period of historical
Analysis was a phase…'—& so, America

Would also prove a phase, one as ice-cubed
Bourbon-brown as a Walnut Manhattan
(With burnt orange tints of angostura bitters),
Or a rained-in balcony's watered ashtrays.

Folk Bartók

Cool summer evenings
Summon piano
Compositions of Bartók
His *non troppo lento*
Cascades somewhere
Between classical & light jazz
His music cleanses
Itself of all psychical
Occupation
Only music can cross
Frontiers of consciousness
Needs no translation—
A universal language
A lingua franca
Melodic glossolalia—

Yet Bartók claimed
Nationalist inspiration
Of Hungarian plain
& Carpathian basin
In folk music
That he & Zoltán
Kodály recorded
On Edison cylinders—

But why try to return
A universal language
To aural Babel again…?

Blavatsky in Violet

"Giantess" of transmigration—in impromptu puffs
Of *"inextinguishable cigarettes"*, Russian tobacco
Self-rolled with origamic finesse: white-eyed
Madame Blavatsky, neé Helena Petrovna
Of the Dolgorukaya dynasty of Novgorod on
The Volga, descended from Carolingian Knights
Of the Baltic-German Mecklenburg line;
Broad head *'surmounted with silver'*, smudges
Of thick curls giving her countenance the patina
Of one of her spirit-portraits palm-rubbed with
Plumbago through a sheet of paper, the self-
Described *"hippopotamus of a woman"* addled
With kidney stones & lumbago (& probably
Tennis elbow), to whom anything of purely
Temporal import was simple *"flapdoodle"*;
Depicted by her theosophical pen-pal, Colonel
Henry Steel Olcott (surname uncannily echoing
'Occult'), his affectionately abbreviated *'H.P.B'*,
"...in her shabby wrapper... smoking cigarettes,
Her huge head with crinkled brown hair bent over
The page she was writing on... a look of introverted
Thought in her light-blue eyes..."; inveterate tester
Of selected friends, Blavatsky had a dragon's
Tongue which *"could breathe enough... fire to... singe*
The green of Holland Park", or scorch the stucco
Of Landsdowne Road, & plenty more residences
Besides; could cause conflagrations across her
Clairaudience sparked to raptures at her
Capacity to magic up crisp bank notes from deep
Within her tobacco basket; producer
Of the transcript, *The Secret Doctrine*, dictated
To her through automatic writing in Seraphic
Purple prose by supreme Tibetan adepts (she,
Their secretary, amanuensis), the resulting
Tome published as a *'door-opener'*—& -stopper—
For scientists all over the globe still *'groping for*
Light at the dead-end of materialism'
As Howard Murphet put it in his biography

Of Blavatsky, the mystically titled *When*
Daylight Comes that materialised through
The Theosophical Publishing House
In 1975 replete with violet-tinted cover
Portrait of la Madame herself (violet
The clairvoyant-colour) & violet-steeped
Photograph of Murphet on the jacket flap—
Signed copies from the other side... & possibly
Now, & forever, over there, Blavatsky is
Enveloped in her vanity project of afterlives,
Violet Unveiled, or *Violet Observed*, revealing
Itself through violet sleeves in violet tropes
On violet-scented notepaper from the violet-
Tinted afterlife, her will still holding out for
That which one of her apostles, W.B. Yeats,
Prefigured as the coming *'greater renascence—*
The revolt of the soul against the intellect'—

O violet emanations, O violet vibrations,
O violet leitmotivs, O violet liquefactions!

O VIKTOR

i.m. Viktor Tausk (March 12, 1879–July 3, 1919)

Some details paraphrased from 'The Influencing Machine', Christopher Turner, *Cabinet magazine*, Issue 14, Summer 2004

With reference to 'On the Origin of the 'Influencing Machine' in Schizophrenia', V. Tausk (1919) and *Four Arguments for the Elimination of Television*, J. Mander (1978)

O Viktor had you survived the pistol & curtain-cord
Of your double-suicide, lived out your natural life
Rather than depart prematurely as a martyr to

Psychiatry, excommunicate of Sigmund's inner-circle,
You would have come to witness the materialisation
Of something uncannily akin to that Influencing

Machine that formed a central concept in your piloting
Paper on schizophrenia, published just prior to
Your leap into oblivion in 1919—named

After the strange glass globe that emitted green light
-ning when rubbed like a genie in a bottle, invented
By Hauksbee, apprentice of Newton's; an umbrella-

Name you gave to such dreamt-up contraptions
Scrupulously pictured by the likes of Jakob Mohr,
& his eighteenth-century precursor, Welsh tea-broker

& architect James Tilly Matthews who named
The machine that tormented him the "Air-loom"—
Both cases exhibited in Hans Prinzhorn's Museum

Of Pathological Art, which you fortuitously visited;
Mohr & Matthews believed they were victims of these
Sadistic devices ("Lobster-cracking" was how

Matthews described the intense mental pressure
To which he was subjected by this cryptic apparatus)
That sapped their vitalities drained by magnetic

Waves they emitted, their minds implanted with
Intrusive images & thoughts against their wills—
O Viktor had you lived you would have witnessed

An invention resulting from experiments by Boris
Rosing, Braun of the cathode-ray tube, Logie Baird
& "Stooky Bill", an Influencing Machine manifest

As a filtering, infiltrating item of furniture
To alter all our realities from the vantage of our
Static-saturated settees: *telephote*, *televista*,

Finally settled as *television*—Jerry Irwin Mander
Would make the link more explicitly in his 1978
Jeremiad petitioning for its elimination on

The basis of its anti-democratic ubiquity
& shaping of public opinion, its manipulating
& puppeteering of our visual & auditory

Senses whilst simultaneously stripping us of smell,
Taste & touch, thus disorienting us, implanting
In our minds alien ideas & false memories

Confabulated from other peoples' experiences,
Psychical warping punctuated by advertisements,
Repeated copywritten prompts: hypnopompic

Capitalism, mass-hypnotism—a parasitic
Portal of marvels & evils & nausea-inducing
Persuasiveness, prone to spread tin foil paranoias—

Phantasmagorias rasterised to rival all
The grandiose grotesque of Robert Burton's byzantine
Anatomy of Melancholy (satirised tangentially

By Laurence Sterne in *Tristram Shandy*), though more
An Anatomy of Banality by the time
Of reality-entertainment: from lofty ambition

Of Reith's didactic set to Bazalgette's septic tank
Of philistinic kitsch... O unhappy Viktor what you
Left behind was a happy accident by which your

Serendipitous description of those antiquated
'Influencing Machines' unintentionally predicted
TV: a device which makes people *'see pictures'*

Like two-dimensional *'hallucinations'*,
That *'produces'* & *'removes ... thoughts & feelings*
By means of waves or rays', that might be termed

"'A suggestion-apparatus'", its *'function'* to transmit
Or drain away vitalities, promote impotency,
Operated by crank-pulling *'persecutors'*, hidden

Persuaders concealed behind a screen—so Viktor,
Your monograph is posthumously repurposed
As an alembic analogue connecting old diagrams

Of *'unimaginable'* engines grown from organic
Imaginations augmented by libido's absence
(Masculinities castrated by *dementia praecox*),

With a polemic on the schizophrenic experience
Of having one's psyche occupied by others,
Or being pulled into others' psyches through

Depersonalised spoon-fed phony-empathy,
Three senses suspended, a spiritual emptying,
Projected into viewers by an ultraviolet box.

Swedish Match

i.m. Hilma af Klint (26 October 1862–21 October 1944)

Hilma af Klint spent enchanted summers
At Hanmora in raptures at natural forms—
But her focus would lift to spirit matters
After her sister Hermina's premature
Matriculation to the afterlife. At twenty,
Hilma went to study Art in Stockholm,
Absorbed by the hub of Blanch's Café;
Abstraction & symbolism fused with spiritism
In her clairvoyant art, geometric astral shapes,
Platonic forms in poster colours;
Kandinsky was, like af Klint, influenced by
Varley's uncanny illustrations for Besant
& Leadbetter's *Thought-Forms*, a study of tulpa—
Which af Klint's byzantine pictures echoed
& complemented; along with Anna Cassel,
Mathilda Nillson, Cornelia Cederberg
& Sigrid Hedman, Hilma formed *"De Fem"*
(*"The Five"*); Theosophy a la H.P. Blavatsky
Was invisible validation—Hilma was
Devastated when Rudolf Steiner seemed
Unimpressed by her output, although
In private he'd kept photographed samples
Of some of her pictures which he later
Coloured in. Hilma immersed herself
In a kind of mediumship: the *"Höga Mästare"*
(*"High Masters"*) guided her hands to produce
Automatic drawings & paintings for
An unexplained *"Temple"* assignment;
Hilma felt her pictures premature,
Needing time to ferment before being exposed
To the unready minds of men—but did
Kandinsky glimpse some via his friend Steiner?
If he did, it puts new light on his epithet:
Pioneer of abstraction in Western Art—
Was Hilma, in fact, that first abstract spark?
Nocturnal channeler of higher powers,

Egoless, she had no thought of her own
Reputation, or posterity, but hid her
Prolific canvases all her life, & in her will,
Stipulated they could only be exhibited
Posthumously & twenty years after her
Passing—up until then, no one living or
Visible had seen them (apart from Steiner,
Kandinsky maybe, her *De Fem* sorority,
& some close relatives in private views).
Now art critics & clairvoyants ask
Was Hilma the Swedish match for
Abstraction, who struck up illuminating
Anthroposophical correspondence
With the Spirit Artists to pilot a new
Perception & consciousness of an objective
& comprehensible spiritual sphere
All around us, pure forms far more than
Figurative but representative of astral
Shapes misinterpreted as simply new
Expressions in the temporal material arts…?

Books Spoken

When my soul broke down, I surrounded myself
In old books & broken clocks with chronically
Faulty tocks, as if I wished to reassure myself
Of something beyond the thin walls' partitions—
Some think spirit knocks are muffled echoes
Of souls passed on attempting to communicate
But on obscure frequencies, faint talk from
Mouths dimmed in the next room… I could no
Longer cope with the violet noise of television,
Too intrusive, that influencing machine;
I couldn't concentrate to read, could only listen
To books spoken—closed my eyes & tried
To immerse in the comforting port-swilled
Claypipe-puffed harrumphs of Tristram Shandy;
The chivalrous soliloquys of sticklike Don Quixote,
His reassuring monologues regaling Sancho Panza
By a Spanish campfire; the submerged digressions
In *Moby-Dick*—polymathic tangents;
The bucolic metaphysics in *The Pilgrim's Progress*
—Heavenly meditations under shady boughs;
Or radio's murmurous otherworldliness,
But barely any music, just trickles of light romantic
Classical, the odd slow sob of chamber jazz…

I was broken, I thought then, beyond repair,
Numbed by sensory overload, imprisoned in
A cramped postage-stamp flat on a road-ringed
Concrete island patrolled by purring engines;
I craved countryside, clean air & silence, felt as if
Perched on a shelf like one of the statuettes
Punctuating the bookcase's rows of warping
Spines like petrified sentries; felt as if the flat
Itself was a Staffordshire Flatback balanced
On the shelf of the street melting into the beige
Stucco's singed meringue, & that I was trapped
Inside it, egg-white, frightened stiff by life,
Feeling everything too intensely, not wanting
Oblivion but to be absent yet aware, but unfeeling,

Be nerveless, invisible, unobserved, an obscure
Book abandoned because it's unreadable,
Bound up in its own unbearable dumbness.

Bed-Written

& you came into my room
& saw all the books
& asked me if I'd read them all
& my eyes swept several shelves
Before I said *"No*
But those I've read I remember well,
& there are even some
I recognise from their smell",
That unmistakable musk of age
That clings like thought to every page
A sweet miasma in a bandage,
& then there are the ones I've written
Which no doubt I'll eventually
Get round to reading one day
When I'm used-up & bed-ridden…

& when I lie dying, around my bed
Will gather guilt & regrets,
All the books I've never read…

Huxley Greys

The Huxley Greys sit accusingly on the shelf,
Jurors of my imagination, their voiceless
Verdict that I lack concentration or can't
Turn off my loud thoughts—but my difficulty
With fiction is more complex: a curse to read
The same lines or paragraphs or pages over
& over again until such point as I feel
Satisfied I've fully absorbed the blood, bone,
Sinew & gristle of the language as it's ground
Through the novelist's ruminating idiom,
Phrases & descriptions, & all this often
At the expense of taking in the actual narrative,
Unmasking the characters, motives & reveals,
Or satisfactorily picturing corporeal souls;
& so I'm cursed by fiction in spite of myself,
A Sisyphan plough through prose as opposed
To sailing a narrative from beginning to end
Without the compulsion to mentally net
& rethread each morphological warp & weft
With the butterfingers of my mind—& it's
Those Aldous Huxley novels I covet most,
Spined in grey eminence, permanently
Impressing on me the sifting time, that I
Must at some point, or counterpoint, pluck
One from the shelf & cast myself adrift
In its lexical textures, attempt to read without
Repeat, repeat, repeat of each well-sculpted phrase,
Focus less on the vocabular fabric,
Not so up close, but trust myself to grasp
The slippery particulars while following the story,
Since it's the story that's supposed to count
The most, no matter how poetic the prose—

But O how words outgrow the thoughts that grow them,
& weigh the pages down to slabs of stone.

Anxiety's Mint

The way, as a family of bookworms,
We used to ruminate over
The most exacting word to describe
Some indescribable problem
That had mushroomed in my mind,
How we'd plough through the language
& its arrangement around
The dilemma's verbalising
Rather than trying to solve it;
There was something almost morbid
In our linguistic scouring,
& I sometimes recognise that it
Was probably on the nubs of these
Verbal symbols my obsessions shrubbed,
On these philological coigns
That my anxieties first spiked,
In these thought-coinages that my
Fixations were first minted.

The Tempting of Parry Amphlett
~~at Penultimate Draft~~

...as if the magic lantern threw the nerves in patterns on a screen
—'The Love Song of J. Alfred Prufrock', T.S. Eliot

'OH I COULD BE GOOD, I COULD BE GOOD—
If I had the strength to be otherwise, I would'
He thought as he stirred his stewed cup of tea
Then, faltering at the thought, appalled,
Placed the teaspoon on the kitchen unit,
Then lifted it towards the cup, then placed it
Down again, then hesitated
Until the morbid thought had grown cloudier—
Then sipped his tea & wished upon his spoon
So engrained with tea-stain, grimed,
'How long will it be until I'm myself again?'—
It seemed so long since the teaspoon shone
& scooped his pale oval face as a cameo—

O WHEN HIS FATHER SIGHS, WHEN HE TALKS OF JUST EXISTING,
Of how sometimes he feels he can't go on,
His soul is tugged down, tugged down with a weight
Into the pitch blackness of a bottomless well—
O he'll still be insisting he'd never actually *do* anything,
Only that he contemplates it sometimes, when alone,
~~Which is pretty much every day for him~~; O
When his father sighs that way & he almost
Pre-empts him uttering his thoughts of hopelessness,
Of bleakness for the future, a future he cannot see—
How many times a day does he also stir a spoon
In his tea ~~(that transfused dark nectar that keeps~~
~~Desperate souls sufficiently stimulated to~~
~~Continue existing)~~ while stewing thoughts dice
With suicide, sugary savage gods of anguish
Dissolving in liquid brown studies…? Like father,
Like son, like Daedalus & Icarus & the sun,
Like Abraham & Isaac & the slab on Moriah,
Like Kierkegaard & Michael the rationalist father—
How they both plough through the grey clod of day
At a distance to one another~~, a distance that aches~~

What ~~on earth~~ is one to do-----------------
About dreams, ambitions, desires, doubts, *you*,
When the day is just something to be *"got through"*?
When each moment is an anguished negotiation
With thoughts' slippery stepping stones to absolutes,
Teetering between extremes, totems & taboos?

Through my fault, through my fault,
Through my most grievous fault

& IF HE THINKS OF SUICIDE, IT'S NOT FOR THE FIRST TIME,
Not even for that day—breakfast, lunch, supper,
Three repasts per day that punctuate the atrophy
Of dismal spirits, though mostly amounting to
Just one unhungry munch from a browning banana—
~~To settle the belly's nausea with potassium—~~
Left half-peeled on the kitchen unit throughout the day
Bruising with the burnisb of long rubbing hours
~~O hours of long choosing & beginning late~~,
Up abrupt with anxious pangs sharp 11 'o' clock shadow,
Pellets for the lugubrious goldfish, bloated
Orange globes, even the bug-eyed Blackamoor
Has long burnished orange as if to camouflage
Himself among the tank's Orandas
Who must presume his bug-eyes are disfigurements,
But as for the horned growth protruding from
His head—if it's an attempted third eye
Then it's a travestied edition

Click of the stove to boil the kettle,
Then the pealing of a ripe banana,
Bite of cream white pulp, then placed back in
The bowl to begin its long-browning into night

'I've simply lost my appetite
for life'

All day bad thoughts grow ram-curls & horns,
Spikes of cropped impulses, barbed doubts,
Arrested urges, nerves never alleviated

Even by rational perspectives arrived at
Vicariously from swerves away from the flashing
Fight-or-flight indicators of the reptilian
Part of the brain—nerves can't be objective;
Nerves, once primed, remain primed, at least until
Some sanity is massaged in with muddy gills
& somehow manages to slither in, like wills...
O we mumble, we mumble in amphiboly...
O but all obsessionals are amphibious souls
Bobbing n' wobbling along: minds half-
Immersed in cloudy kitchen-water, half-
Caked in thinking's thickly caking limescale,
Now the kettle sobs to the boil

O amygdala days are almond-shaped,
& they say the brain smells of bitter almonds /
& at night he eats almond frangipanes
Mirtazapine spawns marzipan cravings

IT'S NOT THE TIMES OF TRAUMA & CRISIS THAT HE FINDS SO DIFFICULT TO GET THROUGH, but the in-between times,
The times of quiet, the times that should be respite,
The un-momentous times, the month-hour moments,
Those moments & times that make up daily life
That he finds the most difficult to get through,
A navigator sans compass, how to negotiate
His way through the small moments, the quiet times
Beset by terrible doubts & catastrophic thoughts
That clutch at his consciousness like thorns or
Brambles or stinging-nettles—O his sanity for
A dock leaf to soothe the itching rash of irrational
Thoughts that just itch more to the scratch—
Insatiable urticaria—allergy to the self

~~*(... & O by the time you read this...)*~~

Perhaps, thinks Parry Amphlett, *for such is his*
Peculiar name ~~so easily compressed to P. Amphlett~~,
I'm tantamount to a martyr of thought,
A faulty plaster saint of scraping grace,

Fundamentally too innocent to amount
To anything of earthly worth—money
Has no moral value, & is merely symbol
Made fungible, it has spending power but no
Spiritual place—too nice to make any success
Of consciousness, good & thus tormented by
Each & every doubt, obsession & suggestion,
A person attempted but abruptly truncated
At the tip of the will, a weak will, perpetually
Tempted by impulses to spill the emptiness
Encapsulated in a pill, pre-empted by
Supreme control, apprehension of consequences,
Moral, emotional, spiritual—& empathy,
Sweet empathy, my poison of compassion,
& the soft hemp ephemeral pleasures that press me
To dispel hope, for hope is what keeps us susceptible
To pain & disappointment, & cope & rope
Are its perfect rhymes, among others, & it takes
A special type of preoccupation to make up tropes

ALL PROTO-AFTERNOONS~~, HIS ARE ALWAYS PROTO-AFTERNOONS~~, are spent catastrophising—this
Is his particular form of automatic thought-penance,
Mental self-flagellation, a peculiar & specific
Mental punishment allotted to him by
Some demiurge which draws energies from his
Psychical pain, long as his lungs tug on cigarettes,
To be condemned to scrimp his life in piles of paper,
Copper pennies & coping stones of poetic powers
Precious consolation to heart-eating anxieties,
Liver-pecked perplexities ~~for fire-eyed forethinkers~~

How is any quality of life to be cultivated
When consciousness is splintered, certainty disintegrated,
Clouded with fogs of false thoughts & feelings,
Compelled into ritualistic behaviours cantilevered
In a cranium cramped by its own imagination?
How to lead any sort of decent life when one's head
Constantly replays the worst thoughts that can be contemplated
Constantly replays the worst images that can be pictured?

What's left to fear for the thus-afflicted…?
~~Against all rationality there's still much to be feared~~

In mornings my nerves devastate
Any benefits of having risen late

It's your nerves, everybody always told him,
That's why you're so sensitive—& you suffer
With your nerves because you are sensitive—
These nerves are his Erinyes

~~*They used to say it was down to the nerves*~~
~~*They used to say it was down to the glands*~~

The thing Parry fears more than anything else
Is having power over other people—
So he prays deep inside:

Give me the power to be powerless
So I cannot do harm, so I cannot grasp,
~~*Slap, stamp, strangle,*~~ *so I cannot destroy /*
Emancipate me from grasping phalanges
~~*Metaphorically*~~ AMPUTATE MY HANDS

Parry puts down on a post-it something punning & allusive:

I am not Orestes
Nerve-the-less
Am pursued by Furies

He rubs each bead of the worry-rosary of his rolling doubts,
Each obsessing bead, neurosis persecutes him
To a cognitive recusant, a neurotic recluse,
Hermitic, a clandestine panic-fiend,
Rigid, all-or-nothing, black-&-white thinking—
He thinks, perhaps happiness is the absence of thought?
Then that must be a kind of death, such mental emptiness,
Such self-emptying as epitomised by the Bethlemite

& do I dare & do I dare & do I dare

To think when every thought is a cross to bear

Don't you know there are thoughts that murder
& there are words that murder themselves
~~Don't you know some words are swords~~
& there are thoughts that beget themselves
~~Don't you know there are cheesewire words~~
~~That garotte with a glottal stop~~

Lord, I am not worthy to receive you under my roof
But only say the word & my soul shall be healed

WHAT WAS IT HIS LONG-LOST UNBELIEVING FRIEND
USED TO SAY BY WAY OF MISANTHROPIC MOTTO:
'Never expect anything, then you'll never be
Disappointed'—such a bitter motto,
Sour tonic for the self-anointed pint-half-empty pessimist,
But his past friend was his soulmate in many ways
(Not to say also soul-antagonist) though they
Clashed, locked antlers from time to time,
His sting-in-the-tail pincering Scorpio
Made sport with Parry's shell-retreating ~~crustacean~~
Cancerian, scuttling crab, Karkinos Καρκινος,
That tries to distract Heraklean consciousness
From its fight with the Thought-Hydra of the mind,
So much of Parry in what he said in spite
Of his recalcitrant insistence at attempting
To still be a Christian, against his mortal atheism,
His implicit conviction that life & everything
In it was ultimately pointless—Parry cannot
Comprehend existence without some numinous
Element, a spiritual purpose; his past friend,
Part alter ego, flipside of the same coin minted
In green fiction, Romantic anticipation,
Pedestals & paper petals, festering lilies scented
Worse than weeds, neurotic roses, neuroses,
Spoilt poetry, &, primed for more disappointment,
He doesn't expect he'll ever see him again,
Nor even know whether he's succeeded
Thus far in resisting the penultimate encap-
-sulation of Seneca's philosophical discipline

~~All his life has been as if spent in an antechamber~~
~~To forbidden pre-emptive embarkation…~~

~~One spends one's entire life~~
~~Trying to pluck up the guts to commit suicide~~

~~Now I commit suicide to paper~~

But, no doubt, like Parry, he's still hooked to cigarettes
That agitate the nerves contrary to past assumptions
(Certes not soothing as hookah-smoking caterpillars)
O those nocturnal sacraments of ~~long~~
~~Twentysomething nights of fired ideas & self-frights,~~
Dreams anticipated & captured up in nets of insights
Never to strike such chords again—
Early risers catch their dreams,
So their late-risers sat up all night & cheated Morpheus
To scoop their catches before tipping into sleep
In impinging curtain-seeping sunlight, smoky vampires

Through my fault, through my fault,
Through my most grievous fault

PARRY. *For myself, so far, I am coping, if precariously,*
& have been spared damnation so far for not
Committing the ultimate sin, the tipping-point
Of despair, self-murder, for want of a more polite
Euphemism, partly Catholic proscription
Has stopped me from that most Protestant act,
It'd be the ultimate insult to Christ—almost
As bad as 'striking God when he's down',
As Henry Scobie puts it in Graham Greene's
The Heart of the Matter, by taking Communion
Without confession & absolution, with sin
Still incubated in the soul, a soupy residue
Of badness unpurged—thus, ceremoniously,
& literally, Scobie damned himself, at least,
Presumed he did, then, more certainly,
Through suicide brought on by a sense of guilt—
His last words, 'God, I love…' ~~*Aren't all the best*~~

~~*Endings open … to interpretation…?*~~

For don't we each, in our own covert, hidden ways,
Commit a little suicide daily ~~(all our days)~~?

PARRY. *& who am I to have that right to take my life*
Which is not mine for the taking & not of my initiating?
No one has that right, ~~*least of all a Catholic,*~~
Our souls are not our property, that's why we spare so
Many thoughts for captives of poverty
& store up such anathema towards their captors,
Those cupiditous property-owners, ~~*capitalistic*~~
~~*Culprits, Herodic powers*~~*—O yes, so far I have been*
Spared from opting out, ~~*since, unlike self-possessing*~~
~~*Protestants,*~~ *I do not see it as an option,*
Only as a hypothetical toy of thought,
Only the atheist can see it as an option & personal right,
As if he had created himself, & owns himself,
& thus has the right to end himself—
But the truth is we have no real choice in it,
Or anything, free will, free choice are egoistic illusions,
Cognitive designs to delude ourselves we have some
Power over ourselves, but if we have, & if free will
& choice are true, then answer this: did we choose
To be born? & do we choose to ~~*one day*~~ *die…?*
I've no truck with choice, I'd sooner be spared this
Dizziness of freedom… Ah, there's the nub of it:
The atheist, nihilist & existentialist each
Wrestles back self-responsibility
By saying that while we do not choose to be created,
To be born, nor choose to be mortal & destined
To death, we can at least choose to end our lives
At a time of our own choosing—Seneca's
Prescription for triumphing over despair
Suicide has haunted me all my life, like a nagging
Shadow ~~*(my soul-word)*~~*, shadow of an albatross,*
Thoughts' cloistered ghost, a poltergeist, a demiurge
Arraigning me with its mad ingrowing greed,
& so many times I've thought I wanted to go
STOP MERRY-GO-ROUND I WANT TO GET OFF!

Due to my morbid obsession with being missed
& mourned by loved ones—at my funeral please
Omit flowers, please omit—ever since I was
An infant I've had an addiction to sadness,
A deep-seated sense of something wrong with
The world & something fundamentally amiss
In myself, I'd like to be missed, to be absent in
Some sense, to be absent but yet be, like thought,
Feeling, faith, belief—& God might well have said:
THOU SHALT KNOW ME BY MY ABSENCE…

But sentience is tricksy & I'm still too attached
To earthly things to leave yet, even if most of
Those things, mostly deleterious, to do with
Literature, my own writing & wish to leave behind
Testaments in print, is construed in preoccupations
With posterity, not to live properly but
To somehow live afterwards, in others' minds,
To haunt life as a ghost then come alive after death,
Anticipating resurrection in someone who's never lived—

Sometimes it seems so sad, so sterile that my ambition
Of being is to be on a spine, my name, that is, P.
AMPHLETT inscribed in some elegant lettering
On a buckram bind, my legacy in lieu of children,
My iambic epitaph in place of pattering feet;
~~Bookbinding glue, my obsolete semen~~;
But still I am kept on this plane of existence
By bonds of love, certain stubborn intimations
To faith of some kind, & a capricious pact which
Just about keeps my faulty soul, ~~splinted spirit,~~ intact:
The chemical trinity: Sertraline, Mirtazapine, Diazepam
Taken daily as sour victuals, chemical sacraments—
& an undisclosed addiction to ~~codeine~~ euphoria

Parry scribbles on a post-it pad by his computer:

My life's a trail of stopped clocks & unconfronted Prufrocks,
The coping stones of years pile up in the pillbox—
Am I a Simon Simplex, a Simple Simon Complex?

~~*So much of my life has been expunged in cigarettes*~~
My thoughts pop like seaweed pods
Crackle to blister packets

~~*O spare me Prufrock's chronic hesitation*~~
~~*But numb me with Mauberley's feebleness*~~

He used to make secretive scribbles on post-it pads
When he felt inspired to poetry in his purgatorial
Office days when he worked soullessly as ~~an~~
~~Emasculated henpecked hunt-&-peck~~ secretary
(Temping, albeit permanently—a permanent
Temp) because he was a fast typist from years
Of writing & publishing some of what he'd written
Though it was all poetry & poetry is an
Impecunious calling, so his daytime occupation
Was in part a means to keeping himself
In his poetry yet paradoxically
He lost most of the time he used to have to compose
Poems when he was unemployed but less inspired

BUT WHAT ARE THESE MERE PILLS & POTIONS
WHEN UP AGAINST TEMPTATIONS?
What use mere alchemy as a safeguard against
Such fundamental powers? Parry's father used to say
To him when he was a boy tormented by horrific doubts,
Ghoulish thoughts & morbid obsessions, that perhaps
He was like one of those Saints constantly
Assaulted by Satan, beset with temptations
Around the clock, night & day, day & night… & yet,
What kind of temptations can these be
That are so repellent for him to contemplate,
That torture him so much, sap his appetite
Until anguished fasting almost becomes a painful,
Stomach-panging monastic way of life…?
The only temptation seems to be in the urge
To let go, lose control, go mad, somehow escape
The captured apprehension, the interminable
Sense of trapped tension in mind, body, muscle,
Bone… He's always felt he needed to escape—

From school, from work, from love, from everything,
Ever since he can remember~~—Houdini of the soul~~…
This is Anxiety as Kierkegaard—that secular Saint
Of angst—depicted it, the anticipation of sin,
The apprehension of uncommitted acts
Nefarious & out-of-character, of moral anarchy,
Hence this deep-seated sense of Catholic guilt
The thorny quilt that gathers round his body
& soul like a rough hairshirt & makes his spirit itch,
His nerves stitch, his muscles twitch, but by itself
Protects him from himself, from what he might
Become but for the ability to project beyond
Acts to consequences & impossibility
Of self-forgiveness after the fault has been
Perpetrated~~—O perpetual *culpa felix*—~~since
How could he then forgive himself if even now,
In this horrendous innocence, this scared
Innocence, he cannot find it in himself to forgive
Himself for simply thinking such unforgiveable things…?
Anxiety is a keyless jailer; Parry must be his own
Confessor, & his thoughts confess hourly
Of their orphaned horrors, aspiring purgatives,
But there is no sense of purgation~~, except by retching~~

Parry Amphletttttt
I whisssssssper in your ear
Go to the cliffffff edge & throw yourselffff offfff ittt
Jusssst like I tempttted the Prophetttt
Go throw yourssssself offff itttt

PARRY WAS ONCE UNHAPPY ACCOMPLICE
TO AN UNPARDONABLE ACT~~, PARTICULARLY~~
~~FOR CATHOLICS~~: not raising an objection to
The termination of something formed from his
Own seed—& he is periodically haunted by this
Unborn incubus, a carbuncle on his conscience (
Though he did confess later to a priest
& received absolution for his obvious remorse)…
They'd taken all precautions, but the rubber must
Have split or had a microscopic aperture,
Or its spermicide misapplied—so it was for

Other post-measures, O pennyroyal pennyroyal—
~~A pill that sounds like a postage stamp—~~
Even that proved impotent in its pre-empting;
& so to the scooped-out womb-pink plush
Of an escape clinic & its implacable purgatives—
She'd been sent shivering into fever, sharp pains
Shooting down, down, & a deep down sense
Of something being pulled out of her, tugged
Out of her, something tiny, immutable,
Imperishable of essence, of soul, if it had a soul
So soon—&, God knows, he hopes it hadn't,
For to pinch out an almost-life is a terrible
Thing, but to put out a soul goes beyond moral
Transgression, becomes its own punishment—
Trapped anathema; & it had been part of him,
Or would have been had it been allowed to grow,
& be born—it was him in miniature,
1/72 of his size, smaller than one of his goldfish,
Much smaller in fact, but somehow similar,
Though more globular ~~(he imagined the embryo~~
~~Bobbing in tank water like a bug-eyed Oranda)—~~
Ever since it had been incubated in the vestibule
Of his troubled conscience, so much so that he
Had gone to confess to a priest & was relieved
For receiving absolution, yet still guilt-ridden

Through my fault, through my fault,
Through my most grievous fault

& HE REMEMBERS HIS OLD SPARRING PARTNER
ON ALL THINGS PHILOSOPHICAL & SPIRITUAL,
Pencil-thin, perpetually unshaven, not so much
A 'friend' as a 'fiend-friend' with whom he shared
Some strange sense of existential fellow-travelling,
They both were seekers after different types of truth,
Thinkers, definitely thinkers, both fascinated &
Frustrated by literature, both aspiring writers, but
Diametrically opposed on metaphysical matters,
Especially when it came to morality &
The concept of spirit or soul, his fiend-friend
A fiercely phrasing, acid-tongued disciple

Of Friedrich Nietzsche~~—*the first thing Nietzsche*~~
~~*Expects of his disciples is for them to reject him!*~~
~~He'd tease—~~at his most misanthropic & anti-
Christian—tasting moralic acid in everything—
& also, more disturbingly, an admirer of Aleister
Crowley & his sex magic; who'd taunt his slightly
Younger God-fearing friend by comparing
Their conversations to the Devil & a Priest
~~(Parry felt had he not been creatively inclined~~
~~He'd have made a priest, or be celibate at least)—~~
If so, his friend was the tempter; not that Parry
Was particularly religious at this juncture,
But he still clutched to the notion of a spirit or
Soul, & the possibility of universal love as
Adumbrated in Christianity, & Socialism
(Its secular equivalent); Parry came to believe
His fiend-friend was 'morally ill', especially
So since his amoral rival seemed to relish his
Sickness so devilishly~~—*All is will to power, will*~~
~~*To power,*~~ (or was it all irony cunningly designed
To wind him up?)—in spite of a certain intense
Seriousness about his manner which would
Normally seem to preclude true wickedness,
So perhaps, in his case, more a philosophical
Quandary; this fiend-friend would mock Parry's
Naivety in believing in universal love,
Fellowship, community, philanthropy,
As anything other than airy-fairy notions
& castles in the air built up like those cramped
Miniature turrets in medieval illuminated
Manuscripts—Parry depicted implicitly
As some monkish scrolling scribe; & yet he
Would treat Parry almost as a disciple whispering
In his ear with ashtray breath, *You've come further*
Than anyone else even if Parry was so patently
Out of simpatico with his fiend-friend's Satanic
Trains of thought—but this came from a scouring
Of Irish Roman Catholicism at its most
Brimstoned & damnatory (so far distant to
Parry's own experience of its watered-down

Englishwashing, still full with incense, guilt &
Confession but not so strict-sounding
When uttered from an English mouth,
As opposed to that feistier & fiercer kind
Of Irish enunciation one associates with stone-
Scouring nuns), which Parry suspected
Had somehow corrupted his fiend-friend's spirit,
Twisted it into barren atheism, moral anarchy,
Often comparing himself to Joyce's Stephen
Dedalus (who then was Parry in this particular
Chapter from *Ulysses*—a blond Leopold Bloom,
A soppy Romantic besotted by beauty
Abstractedly, an almost impotent daydreamer,
~~Frying pig kidneys for Molly's breakfast~~
~~Then dutifully bringing it upstairs on a tray,~~
Putting girls up on pedestals instead of in your bed
As his fiend-friend always said), refusing to kneel
In death-bed prayer by his dying Catholic mother—
Thus, inadvertently, killing her, or something
Spiritually similar, a Joycean *Oresteia*,
Though here the adultery of his Klitemnestra
Was purely spiritual & conducted with
The Holy Spirit—an altogether innocent affair,
& platonic, spiritual; as for his Irish father,
He remembered him in the last stages of dementia,
Dribbling on a peach-spread hospital bed,
Surrounded by other spent vessels ~~*masturbating*~~
~~*So much they drew blood*~~—&, here, in this clinical
Tartarus of senility he'd witnessed the sudden
Wilting of his own sense of faith in anything
Good or kind in anything, for where, he'd ask Parry,
Rhetorically, was his father's soul ~~as he sat there~~
~~Wringing his foreskin of all feeling, bleeding~~
~~& dribbling~~? *His soul had long since departed*
~~*His body*~~ Parry had replied with all the priestly
Sanctimony of someone who'd not witnessed this,
With all the piousness of innocence & wilful
Disbelief in life's manifest indifference
To suffering… His fiend-friend had thus rejected
God, relinquished faith, embraced the material

& visceral; his fiend-friend would place him firmly
As the Camel in Nietzsche's aphorism of the Camel,
The Lion & the Child: the Burdened, the Beast,
& the subsequent morally purged innocent—
& Parry was happy to remain a Camel,
To not unpack his Kipling hump, but keep it
As a cross to bear; Parry could thus prepare
To be another type of martyr

MEANTIME HIS FIEND-FRIEND CONTINUED HIS
HERMETIC PILGRIMAGE OF MORAL ANARCHISM,
Empirical scholarship of hedonism & nihilism,
Stifling himself in the fug of *Silk Cut* incense,
His sacraments, cigarettes, alcohol, aspirin,
Apocryphal promiscuousness, & his only
Self-flagellating tendencies expressed
Through pounding hangovers prolonged
In anti-penitence, more as markers of his
Rakish masculinity, Casanovan virility,
Don Juanesque libertine predilections,
Conducted partly voyeuristically in his digs'
Dinginess, an off-campus Cambodian cave
Where he skulked in his miasma of fag-
Fuelled halitosis, ashtray-mouthed Decadent
With a pornographically sharp intellect,
An undergraduate Kurtz predestined to
A furry tongue, unslakable thirst, effortless First

~~It's not *'to be or not to be'* that is the wrangling quandary,~~
~~But *'to do or not to do'*, or *'to think but not to do'*,~~
~~&~~ Parry spends most of his life trying not to think of doing
What he wants least to do, letting go, losing control,
But to try to not think of something is the surest way of thinking it—
There's the paradox of anxiety in a nutshell,
The Kierkegaardian gourd of angst ~~that's hardest to crack~~

Always that grounding thought which makes him pause before
Slipping out into World through an agonising door;
O how many times is he rooted to the spot by a thought
That stops him in his path, that almost persuades him

To retreat, back into the cramped flat for more ruminating,
To sit it out unfruitfully for the length of a cigarette,
Fathom it before the pluming ash has fallen to the carpet—
O how many times has his spirit phoenix-risen after panic?—
~~Panic, after Pan, Faun-like god of Nature, the wilds, etc.—~~
But it's always an unfruitful pursuit, except for
The mouldering fruit it cultivates for further fruitless
Pursuits of souring thought, bitter fruits of fruitless
Thought, furring & fuzzing over with mould growing
Ever thicker & uneatable, thoughts morbid with mould,
Overgrown ~~with mould~~, mould of greying thoughts,
Bruising thoughts, & the gooey acidic brown residue
Of rotten fruits ~~(like the poisonous oozings~~
~~Of tobacco juice from rain-damp dogends)~~,
Thoughts long-murdered but left to linger on
In some bruised limbo of dark-stained bowl,
A limbo of bowl, a bowl of blue-mould—O
What was it old Prufrock was trying to say?
What was it he meant to say, but never did?
What was the point he never got round to?
Perfect failure, old Prufrock & his coffeespoons

PARRY'S NO PLEASURE IN THE MOMENT FOR ALWAYS
ANTICIPATING THE NEXT MOMENT, & his habits furnish
This sense of never-presentness, in how he rolls his
Cigarettes in advance of smoking them,
Twenty-two slim roll ups lined up in his rusting cigarette case,
~~His lungs have long been rusticating in their burnt-out case~~;

~~It wasn't the cough that carried him off~~
~~But the coffin they carried him off in~~

Every moment is spent negotiating a slippery precipice laced
With eggshells pursued by pincers of self-persecutions
Pacing about the place as if anticipating apocalyptic post,
Soggy dogend-brown envelopes… & every morning
When he puts on his computer to read emails
Expectantly as if they offered vouchers to redeem
Himself from his mental-life—all manner
Of Middle-Eastern heirs to offshore fortunes

Of deposed despots bombard him with their millions:
~~Ms Gaddafi, Ms Hussein, Ms Amini DEARLY~~
~~BELOVEDs~~... Always there's some rugged brand
Seeming to offer redemption, but there's none for
The Damned of Capitalism's Pandemonium,
For those who simply cannot conform to the norm,
Be content just to work & consume—no,
There's no room for dreamers in the coma
Of consumerism, no room for creators in pre-
fabricated reality, realm of demiurges————

Parry puts on a post-it his wilting spirit's advertising
Spiel~~, though far from cupidinous copy~~:

I am not Orestes
Nerve-the-less
Am pursued by Furies

Or is he the progenitor of Oedipus, ~~swellfoot,~~
Attempting to obviate the feared event
That obsesses him like a perverse addiction
Which gives him no pleasure or respite but
Yet fixes to his nerves like an adhesive,
By apprehending it, anticipating it, pre-empting it
Mentally...? That's anxiety: guilt without the act

Kierkegaard, Kierkegaard,
His name Danish for Churchyard—
A surname draped in covert pastoral—
His father, beneath prosaic 'rustic
Cloak' was also philosophical

& O HOW HE HATES CAPITALISM'S SPIRIT-SAPPING
ECONOMIC TRAP THAT PUTS A PRICE-TAG
On everything, imprisoner of compassion &
Authentic personality, emancipator of animal spirits,
~~& its accomplices,~~ consumerism & commoditisation—
Human relations reduced to mutually cheating transactions,
Profiteering at others' expense, oneupmanship (
Parry's favourite episode in the New Testament

Was when Christ lost his temper in the temple
& drove out the moneylenders ~~to the scourge of small cords~~);
Perhaps Parry's nervous disposition, extreme sensitivity,
His proneness to morbid obsessions, is his brain's way
Of rebelling against materialism? ~~What else are~~
~~Commodities but thoughtforms personified~~
~~& humanised by demonic copywriters while~~
~~The workers who produce them but who cannot~~
~~Afford to buy them are dehumanised to objects?~~
~~Objectified… while objects are reified, deified,~~
~~Ensouled while their producers are scooped of souls;~~
~~Property & possessions become conspicuous~~
~~Unctions, scourge of socialist compunctions~~

The etymology of obsession is the Latin *obsessus*,
To be besieged, & O he's besieged on a daily basis,
Habitually, by his own interminably rumbling mind;
A vertiginous mosaic of spiralling ruminations
A byzantine mind
A Byzantian mind
Byzantian byzantine
~~Byzantine Byzantian~~

~~*(…& O by the time you read this…)*~~

The etymology of obsession is the Latin *obsessus*, *to be besieged*,
& O he's besieged…

(…& O by the time you read this…

~~The etymology of obsession is the Latin *obsessus*, *to be besieged*,~~
~~& O…~~

…my nerves are bad, especially in the mornings…

(…& O by the time you read this…
I will be bobbing oblom in blooms of green algae)

…& O…

~~*…to be is to be besieged…*~~

~~*…by the time you read this I…*~~

…guilt in everything I think & do…

…& O…

…by the time you read this…

~~*…& O…*~~

~~*…stop merry-go-round I want to get off…*~~

…& O…

…by the time…

~~*…stop merry-go-round I want to jump off…*~~

…& O…

~~*…by the time, by the time…*~~

…& O…

…the time

~~*(…& O by the time you read this*~~

~~*Etc…)*~~

Margate Fragments

A Supplemental experiment

Details paraphrased or included as found text and excerpts from Matthew Hollis's *The Waste Land—A Biography of a Poem* (Faber & Faber, 2022)

1. *La Salon*

What characters he had known—

Iris Barry would often document them
From the vantage of her Chelsea rooms
Literary salons in sundry restaurants

Loquacious Violet Hunt peeling snails
From her Gaudier-Brzeska garden bust
Of Ezra Pound

Eliot depicted as Prufrockian clerk
Unable to break any ice

May Sinclair 'dark-eyed, crisply spoken'
Conspicuous in 'raspberry pink'

Ford Maddox Ford, moustachioed, stentorian

H.D. sat hauntedly next to her uniformed
Husband Richard Aldington (c. 1917)

Harriet Shaw Weaver of *The Egoist*,
An arch-hatted highly strung upright

John Rodker of Ovid Press accompanied
By 'vermilion-haired Mary Butts', his printer wife

W.B. Yeats awkwardly sipping soup
A stray black lock flopping into the bowl

Each time he stooped
& feline Ezra Pound with his 'greenish cat-eyes'
& flaming red hair
Constantly clearing his throat—
'red-bearded, blue-eyed 'Nordic blond''
In 'tengallon hat'—

CALLING CARDS
St John & Mary Hutchinson of Hammersmith
Clive & Vanessa Bell
Aldous & Maria Huxley
Middleton Murray & Katherine Mansfield
(Riveted observing kiwi coquette)
O how evenings wore on
Ottoline Morrell, 'Mary Hutch & Eliot'
Etc.

2. *Les Chambres*

18 Crawford Mansions, Homer Row, Marylebone W1,
Cramped three-bedroomed apartment
Of Mr & Mrs T.S. Eliot

Black & white-striped wallpaper in the hallway,
Orange in the dining room-cum-study
Where T.S. worked at his PO-E-TRY
His desk chair with its back to the fireplace

A 'small iron balcony' where one might contemplate
Suicide intermittently each day,
Just high enough to jump from
& probably break something chronic

Nervy Vivien nicknamed the place
'Eliot's remote tower'
With an acid affection, her 'wilderness'

O Vivien's nerves

Her evening nerves especially
Eliot confided in Brigit Patmore
No rest cures sufficient for her psychical recusancy

This 'mental instability' was 'inheritable'
In Vivien's family
So she had been reared to believe
Brought up on bromide
Prone to migraines
The brain *"grumbusking"*
Like Genghis Khan
In Mongol-like sweep
Of the plains of consciousness

Down below in the street they'd observe
The 'boisterous Laurie Arms public house'
"a little noisy corner, with slums & low streets
& poor shops close around"

The Eliots' maid, Ellen Kellond, their own
Domestic ventriloquist
Of working-class pub gossip
Cue Albert and Lil
(Who'll be heard from later)

T.S. once complained about the upstairs 'actresses'
Who played a gramophone at full pitch in the night
& was told by the landlord it was down to
Their "Artistic Temperament"—O irony

Cramped apartment, in disrepair, & far too noisy
For any poet to hear themselves poeticise

O for some peace

Sometimes for light relief Eliot depicted
Himself & Pound as 'Eeldrop' & 'Appleplex',
Alter egos, mystic & anthropologist
Studying the lower classes as they
Tapped their cigarette ash from the balcony

3. *The perambulatory Pounds*

At Pound's pad, 5 Holland Place Chambers,
'a gloomy and chilly three roomed' stucco-igloo
"designed by an imbecile or an Eskimo''—

Pound perched at a small triangular desk
In the corner of the compact pentagonal room

No space was too cramped & inappropriate
For Pound to spout forth—
He'd once 'removed his pince-nez in a Kensington
'bun shop' in 1912' to declare to Aldington
& H. D. that they were 'Imagists'

Pound elevated three contemporary writers
As "In the Vortex"—himself (of course),
The "man with a leaping mind'' (Eliot),
& caprine bespectacled Joyce who was however
"Utterly out of their compass"

(Wyndham Lewis brought up the rear)

Together they formed 'the "opposition"'
(taxonomist Connolly's literary 'Mandarins')
To the mouldering 'episcopate
Of the corpses of official English literature'

& their spiritual correspondents? Sextus Propertius,
Laforgue, Baudelaire, Homer et al

They all liked their tipples but could be drunk under
The table by E. H. (Eileen Harriet) Anstruther

Mauberley's was a jar half empty
'a life not grasped'—
But more on him anon

*

Some time later the Pounds moved to
70 bis rue Notre-Dame-des-Champs
Close to Luxembourg Gardens
'insulated from the street'
By "two rows of building"
Down an alleyway that 'opened on
a pavilion courtyard of small trees
and a crumbling statue of Diana and the hound'—

Far from the Alpine Lac Léman
Where trees kissed by the wintry Alpine air,
Its 'bitter Bise', turned to ice sculptures—

Furnishings: a low Oriental-style red tea table,
& a 'triangular typing table', Gaudier-
Brzeska paintings on the wall, 'suitcase-
sized clavichord' Pound had 'commissioned
from Arnold Dolmetsch'

Above them lived—or rather existed—
Opium-addicted Detroit poet
Ralph Cheever Dunning, nicknamed
For his reclusive lifestyle by Ford
Maddox Ford 'the living Buddha of
Montparnasse'', no one ever saw him
Speak or eat, as if he had no mouth,
Hermitic aesthete, 'his spartan apartment
had just a single chair, a stove, a bookcase
and a cot', Bodley Head had published
'a slim collection of poems' of his
In 1910, & he'd 'spent the next decade
trying to perfect a second book ...toast
of Parisian conversation when in
1925 he was awarded *Poetry* magazine's
Helen Haire Nevinson Prize',
But by 1930 Dunning was
Consumed by tuberculosis

4. *2635 Locust Street*

Eliot had come far from Locust Street,
St Louis, Gloucester, Massachusetts, steam & heat
'soot-covered, choking buildings'

Realm of the 'yellow smoke' that choked Prufrock,
& of the 'purple shadows of Sara Teasdale's
'Sunset: St. Louis''—she had attended
The Mary Institute next to the Eliot
Family home on Locust St.

Ragtime had started here where Scott Joplin
Composed 'Maple Leaf Rag',
He was de facto 'King of Ragtime',
Musical patron of 'ragpickers'—
This was the 'first African American music
to find acceptance in white society'—

It barrelled out from 'honky-tonk bars'

'The Cubanola Glide'
St Louis brewers Anheuser-Busch
Eliot's burning bantam ears embarrassed by banter at the bordello door

Intemperate city
Smuggling & speakeasies & rum-running &
Bootlegging: boy Eliot used to watch
Schooners sailing into harbour with cargos
Of contraband liquor in burlap-wrapped crates
Under guard of Colt-Browning machine guns

& nearby, the rumbling brown sibilant river,
Miss-is-si-ppi,
Old watery haunt of Mark Twain where
He'd set Huckleberry Finn adrift—old
Rumbling 'Big Muddy'
A 'strong brown god'

2635 Locust Street—
Roomy, decorous eaves, wooden porch,
Imposing almost Gothic brick façade looming
Over the street like a daunting antediluvian
Relative bolt upright at the breakfast table—
Pillar of the community of clapboard houses

William Greenleaf, distaff grandfather, founder
Of the local Unitarian Church—
Eliot told Emily Hale, his Hyacinth Girl, in a letter:
"We lived practically in a slum", or at least,
"shabby to a degree approaching slumminess"

Locust Street as its name suggested
Was a pestilence of yellow smoke
'lit by dim gas lamps, and by brighter Welsbach
mantles which emitted an incandescent white light'

But the Eliots endured: their family motto:
'*Tace et fac...*: Be quiet and do'—
Most unPrufrockian in its distinct absence
Of hesitation—
Home was where one must 'Curl up
the small soul in the window seat /
Behind the *Encyclopaedia Britannica*'

O Animula

In the Gorgonic grotto of the local schoolyard
There grew 'a large ailanthus tree of heaven,
a scrub tree renowned for growing through concrete
dereliction, and for its 'rank' odour''
Of something rotting
Or maybe sulphur

Eliot self-described: 'a lazy idle fuddler... hustled)
by one or another of a crowd of shadows'

Boston scene—
Symbols

Cymbals
'object correlatives'
To 'stir the emotive response' of readers
Such emotive symbols were 'the faded
poor souvenirs of passionate moments'—
Or their anticipation
As Prufrock & his coffee spoons

5. *Lampoonery*

Eliot lampooned impossibly posh Betrand Russell
As 'Mr Apollinax'

Pound lampooned the likes of Aldous Huxley
As having undergone a ''Bloomsburial'' of abilities

A.R. Orage
Olga Rudge

Far from the "gadding mind"
Far from the gadding crowd
& Pound's pallid apparitions in the streets:
'*Petals on a wet, black bough*'

Virginia Woolf at a rainy Trafalgar Square
Described the swarming crowds as 'a cluster
of drenched bees'

'objective correlative', if you please

Sydney & Violet Schiff
Eleanor Hinkley

Eliot ground down by the demands of dinner parties
Sparring & ripostes more precision-based than fencing

Théophile Gautier—*touché*
O Hippopotamus

Pound pointed out Eliot had 'modernized himself
on his own' even if his poetry
Had been partly hammered out in the smithy
Of the Symbolist 'shadow of Jules Laforgue'—
Laforgue's forge, as it were

Was Prufrockian Eliot uxorious? Was he,
Heaven forfend, a cuckold?
Bertrand was detectably up to something
With Vivien in her husband's absence
(Though could well have been even in his presence)—
Or so Bertrand's fictional outings hinted,
His Mr Quantox to Eliot's Mr Ellerker

Uxorious Mr Ellerker
Cuckolded Mr Ellerker

6. *Bosanham*

Ancient site of a 'humble monastery'
Originally called Bosanham
Now Bosham

'twas here apparently King Canute
Sat as the waters lapped at his feet
& wrapped round the legs of his creaking throne
To prove a 'limit to his omnipotence'
In being unable to command the incoming
Tide to turn back

Now Eliot, a rackety Canute
From across the Pond
Boston Brahmin
Taking his cure at Bosham
Wetting his toes
In the pavement-lapping water
Rackety Corona typewriter
Cradled in his trousered lap

Raptackle Barn
Picnic with Vivien
Nerves & *vol-au-vents*
Overlooking Bosham's
Deep 'green silence'

Betweenthem

7. *O Corona*

Prufrock had been typed up
In 'splendid purple italic on a Blickensderfer'
Then submitted to 'a hierarchy of marking'
& a scattering of lines

Scattered chalk escarpments
'rough manuscript in Itchenor'

Maha-Vagga
& a lava ashtray

O Eliot composed upon the typewriter
His nerves as jaded
As his screeching Corona
Thoughts pattering at pica pitch

His 'wretched' old Corona typewriter
Hailed from Harvard days c. 1914
'carried over in his suitcase'
Across the slaty Atlantic
Carried over like the carriage return

O wretched ol' Corona typewriter
O rackety ol' Corona typewriter

[Pound possessed a 'Corona 3 portable
model on which the platen carriage folded
neatly over the keyboard after locking

the escapement throwout']
Now to the long project in hand
Working title lifted from Dickens' *Our Mutual Friend*:

HE DO THE POLICE IN DIFFERENT VOICES.

O Enobarbus
'Excideuil was a troubadour'

'Gerontion'—Eliot was old before his time
Goodbye Piccadilly, Farewell Leicester Square
Fairwell Antwerp, its bustling estaminets
& Brussels-blistered ashtrays

How Eliot alliterated lists of names
'De Bailhache, Fresca, Mrs Cammel'

'Immature poets imitate, mature poets steal'

Cantabrian sun temple
What a spot for Pound's *Cantos*

8. *Sulphur Baths*

Occitanie—to take a rest cure
'a restorative course of 'sun, air & sulphur bath'
in the mineral waters at nearby Brive'
Under Pound's supervision
See the sights
Byzantine tower
Basilique Saint-Front
Font de Gaume cave
Not so much a holiday as a pilgrimage
O Magdalenian draughtsmen
Rock drawings
'tracing the wave-like carvings'
Here Eliot confided in Pound
Of his conscious horror of the prospect

Of an afterlife
Of a spiritual waiting room for eternity
Wracked with angst & unbreakable ice
Awkward silences
Purgatorio
Purgatory
Where souls indulge optional suffering
For purpose of purgation of all impurities
& there is hope in this

& yet Eliot was frightened of life
& would 'look to death for what life cannot give'—
Eliot: 'There are moments ... when
a man may be nearly crushed by the terrible
awareness of his isolation from
every other human being'—
''This sense of dispossession by the dead
I have known twice,
at Marlow and at Périgueux''

Spiritual dispossession
A casting out:
'a confiscation of occupancy, of property or land'
From the Deuteronomic word *yarash*:
'to seize, inherit or disinherit, drive out,
to become impoverished or brought to ruin'

Self-purgation of ego: 'The progress
of an artist is a continual self-sacrifice,
a continual extinction of personality'

9. *Londinium*

'One remains always a foreigner' in London
Unreal city

Vivien had found Eliot 'dishevelled' & 'more volatile'
On his return from France

He would frequently leave her with her evening nerves
To stew in tea-infused juices
(They blackberried after dinner with the Hutchinsons)

Poetry was Eliot's escape from personality
'''Poetry is not a turning loose of emotion,
but an escape from emotion; it is not
the expression of personality,
but an escape from personality''

Poetry was Eliot's opium against pain

To Pound, religion grew 'thought-mould' in the mind

'Brahma's *Da, Da, Da* in the Hindu Brihadaranyaka'
Datta. Dayadhvam, damyata.
Maha-Vaggā
Madame Sosostris
Whose own demise is 'marked upon the cards'
Like Cleopatra

Eliot had thought some of Pound's Cantos
A 'rag-bag' of 'reticent biography'
Hugh Selwyn Mauberley
(Dreamt up by Pound as 'an impossible poet')
Published by Ovid Press—
Epigraph: *The heat calls us into the shade*
(Might have been Eliot's motto)
Source: Nemesianus, third-century
Foreign-resident of Rome, where he
'flourished', probably

Carthaginian in origin
Mauberley was 'not, not assuredly alabaster'
Not memorialised in marble
He dodged the Great War
In which millions of young men had perished
'For an old bitch gone in the teeth,
For a botched civilization'

The Rhine, the Danube, the Elbe, the Oder
Eliot knew that poets were part of a continuum:
"the great poet is prolonging the work of the people
who preceded him, and laying out the work for
those who follow him; the greater the poet,
the more evident his hand in every line,
and the more elusive his personality"

Eliot's erstwhile friend who later
Felt let down by him & who'd write
Elsewhere that Eliot was devoid of feelings
But 'disgust, despair and suicidal impulse'
& Aldington's opinion from having
Trawled *The Waste Land*: 'After that
the only thing for us all to do now
is to go home and commit suicide
as painfully as possible'

Or take some pills 'to bring it off'

While, with a comparable despair, but one
Oppositely borne of unbounded admiration
Of the great work, Pound felt he & other poets
Might as well now 'shut up shop'
After having been exposed to this poem
Of 'permanent value'

Eliot had been a tough negotiator
With various editors, publishers & journals
In the pursuit of advances
& had even argued time spent fine-tuning
One work for publication had prevented him

From penning other works he might
Otherwise have written:
'That was a new kind of thought for any
publisher to be expected to absorb:
that they might reward a writer for
a discernment that made their work valuable
in its rarity: that in effect they might
reward a writer not to write'

His explosive poem,
Supreme poem,
Would make ripe pickings for critics,
& scraps for lickspittle sycophants—
"a great many jackals swarming about waiting
for my bones"

Hence Eliot had reinforced the poem
With extensive notes that picked apart
Its myriad allusions & references
By way almost of deconstruction
Used also as preventatives to denigrations,
'spiking the guns of critics', proleptic
Ripostes to anticipated criticisms

The poem's inscription:

for E. P.
miglior fabbro
from T. S. E.
Jan 1923

Aldington admonished Eliot as 'bitter
& hypercritical'

Eliot would constantly have to police
The alternating title of his work:
Not "Waste Land" but "*The* Waste Land"
Not "The Wasteland" but "The *Waste Land*"—

But had the title, in any case,
Been reappropriated from 'Waste Land'

'(which may have been a misprint for 'Wasteland')',
A poem of 1913 by Madison Cawein
The 'pool-hall poet of Louisville'
Nicknamed "the Kentucky Keats"

Fresca couplets had been replaced
By Tiresias
& the typist with her bedspread of tins

But Phlebas had to stay according to Pound
He was the anchor of the poem

Vivien: "Tom is having a bad nervous –
or so called – breakdown ... In a short time
I hope he will go to Switzerland,
to see Dr Vittoz"

Here Julian Huxley & Ottoline Morrell
Had taken their cures
For similarly numbing
Mental ailments—
Huxley communicated
A 'calamitous state when any mental effort,
and any attempt to reach a decision, even
in trivial matters, becomes a source of anguish',
while Morrell explained simply
Her feelings felt temporarily dead—
Together they found
Their Magic Mountain

Vittoz taught techniques of mentally
Eliminating letters from words in effort
To 'remove destructive thoughts'—
Ottoline's daughter would remark
When observing her mother 'staring
into space: 'There is Mummy
eliminating"—Vittoz' technique
Attempted 'to intercept thought
and create a quarantine for emotion'

This was a psychical house-cleaning
An exercise in 'mental hygiene'
The poem, or rather, the poetic fragments
Unearthed by Eliot had taken time to assemble
Were unfinished from Switzerland
'a sculpture half-emerging from its marble'

10. *Vivien Observed*

Katherine Mansfield didn't take to Vivien
When the Eliots visited her & Middleton
Murry at their Hampstead pad,
Especially when Mrs E was pluming away
On her bedroom sofa—
She couldn't stand 'this teashop creature'
Who'd send "the whole room quivering"

Hope Mirrlees saw in Vivien
A haunted ghost

Vivien would indeed in time be betrayed
& left bereft feeling 'thrown,
pained and 'absolutely alone''
Eventually taken to a nursing home
After fugues wondering nighttime streets
Padding round Paddington in bare feet
Stricken with *Streptococcus fecalis*,
Frequently suicidal,
& ultimately committed
Where (probably by bromide)
The recommended regimen was simply:
'She must be made to sleep'

'Who is the third who walks ^always^ besides you?'

Who leaves no footprints
No patter of tiny feet…
'But it is terrible to be alone with another person'

Two peoples' presence in absence
Thomas & Vivien
Evening nerves
In the violet hour
Dusk depressions
Playing chess
Only ivory men between them
'fugue of a couple'
Only human touch warms up cool ivory

Tired children light sensitive

My nerves are bad tonight.

No issue, no issue
''*Est-ce qu'il n'a pas d'enfants?*' Has he no children?'
'*Il est eunuque, a s'entend.*' He is a eunuch, of course.''

As Lil would echo:
'What you get married for if you don't want to
have children?'
& the pills 'to bring it off'

Phantom children
Ghost offspring
Never to spring from their loins
Faintly heard whimpering in a corner—
'the undetected presence in the apple tree'

The unhappy marriage would even be
Lampooned by Richard Aldington

Disintegrating marriage

'arid places of April', breeding
Aridness, barrenness

Yet after her death Eliot had experienced
A death in terms of his imagined love
For his Hyacinth Girl, Emily Hale,

Which he now realised had always been
A phantom of the heart,
'the love of a ghost for a ghost'
Consummated by post

'neurotic carnality'

Fleshwise he'd had a brief dalliance
With Nancy Cunard when she popped by
London from Paris for a sojourn
Suppered together at Percy Street
Then caressed in the Wyndham Lewis Room
But it left a bitter 'taste of ashes'
In Thomas's smoky mouth

'*Co co rico* the cockerel crows'

Come in some company
Shakespeare & Company
Come in Mrs Equitone, Madame Sosostris

Bloomsbury
Paris
Left Bank
Picasso, Braque, Matisse, Apollinaire, Picabia
At the literary court of Gertrude Stein
La salon de litterateur
Laced with coffee, chicory & ichor
& countless pluming cigarettes

After an impromptu dance
Ezra 'flicked the cigarette girl aside'

11. *Critical Receptions*

Ara Vos Prec variation appeared
With Ovid Press 1919

Eliot's *Poems* from Hogarth Press 1919
'Prufrock's dedication to Jean Verdenal ... restored'

The *Times* was scathing, even manslaughtering:
'a grubby verse of 'endlessly recurring squalor'
by an author 'fed up' with life—and if fed up,
it posited, then 'why write verse about it; why not
commit suicide?''—old Seneca's dictum—
'(Eliot could at least now join Pound in
Their critical invitations to self-harm.)'

The *Observer*: 'The irony of things-as-they-are
haunts the poet as it haunted his forerunner
Laforgue ... and levies board-wages upon all
his emotions'

Pound and Eliot were both accused of 'merely
clever, very very clever' verse
Of being elliptic, esoteric
Pound had no time for 'tump-tump' pentameters
Much less rhyme
For him Harold Monro & his Georgian school
Were anathema—
He might imagine Monro as a lugubrious
Goblin marbleised in 'thought-mould'
(Though Monro was much more than a Georgian)
Pound would use 'georgian' as a prime insult
He'd sometimes pencil it in 'damningly
in the margins' by lines of Eliot's
To pinch him awake whenever he lapsed
Into teapot-spouted poetry

O O O O Harold Monro
More of a poet

Than anyone could know
'Chiral clockwise'
Roland Garros

W.C. Blum hammered Pound's *Instigations*
Published by Boni & Liveright
"Who is Blum?? nom de Plum, nom de Blum?"
Pseudonym of James Sibley Watson
For Pound "a pearl among publishers"
W. C. Blum
W.C. '"buncumb"
Pound slept on Catullus' 'parlour floor'
In Sirmione where he swore
He felt 'forgotten gods moving', arranging
The weighted furniture

Son of one Homer Loomis Pound
Whom 'as a young boy he followed ...
into work at the grand old Philadelphia
Mint on the corner of Chestnut and Juniper,
behind white marble frontage—
the impression of its '"Greek temple" façade"
not lost upon young Pound'

Boyhood hours spent in the crouching shadow
Of his father 'working under natural light
like an alchemist in his cavern to measure
to one-thousandths the proportion of golds
in his cylindrical bottles; hours seated
at his father's roller-top yellow desk
with its two dozen drawers and cubby holes,
its assortments of... government gold,
and blank coin discs yet to be pressed into value'

Carlyle said the poet was a 'Hero-soul'
Pumped with 'the blood of the hecatombs'
All except feeble Mauberley
"Him of all men, unfit"
So much for "osmosis of body and soul"
More osmosis of obsolescence

Through the 'bleating centuries'
All poets know
"the only hope of fame is posthumous"

Maxwell Bodenheim
Madame Ludmila Bloch-Savitsky
Shakespeare & Company
Robert McAlmon
Sherwood Anderson
Sydney Waterlow
Faber & Gwyer
Faber & Faber
Where as editor Eliot would fly far above
The petty peccadillos & fetishes
Of a pedestrian public lapping up
Georgian averageness of verse
Ombrophilous Monro
Glowering under his upturned umbrella
Even now rubbished his own shrubs
Lascelles Abercrombie was now "turgid",
Wilfrid Wilson Gibson "facile",
Robert Graves, John Drinkwater & D. H.
Lawrence "insufficiently profound,
specious and wearisome" respectively—
Georgianism had been
Harold Monro's "middle-class smudge"
Something was needed to revivify
"the worn nerves and arthritic limbs
of our diction" (E.P.)

Mr. T.S. Eliot Esq
'Banker, Critic, Poet'
"pale, marmoreal Eliot"
As V. Woolf framed it
Depicting the vampiric poet, 'She
reported a rumour circulating
in Bloomsbury that Eliot was now
applying violet powder to his face
in order to make him look 'cadaverous';
she described his mood as 'slightly

malevolent', and said that she wasn't
sure that he did not also paint his lips'

He was perpetually on
The precipice
Of 'complete physical breakdown'

In 'The Romantic Englishman'
Eliot remarked how our lace-collared
Scowling seventeenth-century
Forebears had 'fewer prohibitions'
To contend with
(Though no doubt more inhibitions)
At least they weren't polluted
By 'the petrified product which
the public school pours into our
illimitable suburbs'

12. *Albert & Lil & Ellen & Will*

Albert & Lil were
'pure Ellen Kellond'—
When Ellen's husband
William Sollory
Lost his position as
Foreman in a metalworks
Eliot negotiated
Labour exchange payments for him—
Sollory to Eliot:
"I only wish I could be of some service to you
in return." But then Ellen already had been
With her spontaneous spoken
Transcriptions of pub-life

The saloon bar, the music hall,
Yes the music hall—just as old John
Davidson had evinced back in
The Yellow Nineties was a source

Of unvarnished cultural vitality,
Visceral vernacular, anecdotal idiolect,
Even expletive, which could revivify
& lift the heavy weighted velvet
Of Victorian verse, its moth-eaten
Tennysonian sepulchral poetics—

Eliot: "Perhaps the music-hall comedian
is the best material"
I say I say I say
Pub gossipers
Saloon bar cards
Characters of comedy revues, music hall, cinema
Would 'provide fragments of a possible English myth'
Seneca had pioneered this
With his minstrel troupes
'rising in turn each to do his "number", or varying
their recitations by a song or a little back-chat'—

I say I say I say...
Did you hear the one about the emperor & the pumpkin?

Eliot & Pound as doubleact 'Cibber' & 'Cholmp'
Present:
Apocolocyntosis—
The Pumpkinification of (the Divine) Claudius
Music-hall style

'The flicker of a moving picture, the jump
of a gramophone needle, the rapid revolve ...
'the wireless' (Stravinsky noted that Eliot
had a fondness for such 'horse-drawn phrases'
as 'the wireless')'—the poem & its atmospherics
compared to 'listening to stations on a long-wave
radio while tuning the dial between them'

*'the rapid and unexpected combination of images
apparently unrelated'*

'A heap of broken images'

Fossils, crocks, shards, sherds
Margate fragments

Symphonies, counterpoints, absolute music

'cine-reel of a disappearing Europe'

Magic lanterns
'capacity for damnation'
Shadow theatres splattering
'continuous physical horror' of politics

13. *Rescues & Rest Cures*

Poetry & criticism
Interlocutory disciplines
'Criticism is the chamber of poetry;
how the room is arranged is the poem'
Critical prospectuses
Cropping up like crocuses
'*A new poetry that flowers on the stem of the oldest.*
An original cadence. An inventive form.
A distanced intimacy. A music hall
in which all that was missing was
the discovery of cadence and tempo'

'The poet is the smith at the poem's forge;
the poem is the heated metal; criticism
is the anvil over which the object is shaped;
when it is cooled, it is for the reader to determine
the sensory significance of the artefact.'

Shirehampton Public Hall
Bosham Harbour
Bosham Hards
Camber Sands
Unreal

Something for Vivien to absorb her mind in
Breakdowns & bootstraps
Pull her up pull her up

Sometimes their breakdowns would clash:
Vivien: "Tom has had rather a serious breakdown
... I have not nearly finished my own nervous
breakdown yet."

Garsington manor house of
Ottoline Morrell
Said Henry to Mother Eliot:
'('Vivien always recites some account of her
migraines'...)'
they 'lingered on at Wigmore Street 'morosely''

'By the end of September'
The versifying banker had 'overdrawn
his nervous energy'
He required a 'leave of absence'
'medical regimen of rest, diet and repair'

To Pound the English tended to 'terminate
'below the cervical ganglion''

'Four months of flat-hunting' climaxed at the feet
Of an "insane she-hyaena" landlady
Clattering gate of Clarence Gate Gardens
With American-style elevator

A migration beyond 'busy Marylebone Road'

Eliot took a break after the latest exhausting move
Reuptaking an apartment in Paris
'pension near the Panthéon' he'd once shared
With Monsieur Verdenal
Whose attention he'd once gained only by
Throwing a lump of sugar from his window
Overlooking the garden
Politics? Don't talk to Eliot about politics:

"The whole of contemporary politics etc. oppresses me
with a continuous physical horror like the feeling
of growing madness in one's own brain"—
Better tittle-tattle of teapot politics
Eliot was a political apostate

Catholicism beckoned
Or at least High Anglicanism
& Carlism
As in Spain
& the Classics
(They never went away—
Sempiternal—always relevant)
& the dictum of Charles Maurras
'classique, catholique, monarchique'

All else was desolation
'desuetude'

Pound would point to Eliot's 'parsimony'
"He is now respected by the Times Lit. Sup.,"
'buncomb' to think poetry required a moral code

Joyce's *Ulysses* had consumed nine typists—
The eighth threatened suicide from the balcony

Pounds epithet for the inaccrochable
Commodious magnum opus: "enormous –
megalo-scrumptious – mastodonic"

Eliot: "But otherwise, I have nothing but admiration;
in fact, I wish, for my own sake, that I had not read it."

Time to 'shut up shop'
Just as Harold Monro would do—?
Behind his back curtain
At the Poetry Shop
With a polite wave of his hand

No, not for Eliot

12 rue de l'Odéon
Boulevard Saint-Germain
Saint-Sulpice
'dust and tumult of Lombard Street'
Gandon's elegant building burnt down
To a blackened carcass
Tiresias seer of Thebes
"young man carbuncular"
Poisoned by the water in Tilphussa's tainted spring

14. *The Desert Year*

Blooming friendship with Aldington in Margate
'during [Eliot's] breakdown and recuperation'

Portuguese Man o' War washed up
On Margate beach
Poisonous squids & octopi

'the grasses of Thanet were parched'

'patchwork of yellow and brown, dried tubers. Autumn
continued as if summer would never end: the desert year'

Oasis at Albemarle Hotel,
Margate—sought by J. M. W. Turner
For its 'unrestricted light and skies'
'the loveliest in all Europe', but the early
Victorians came 'escaping from a chrysalis
state in London to flutter as
a butterfly at Margate''

Anna Pavlova & Nellie Melba
At the Winter Gardens—desserts,
Raspberry Pavlova & Peach Melba

'thrill-screams' and 'gulls' the sounds of the town
The scenic railway against the Margate skyline

Fun for all the family at Dreamland
Heartbeat of Margate
Margate Sands
Send a postcard

Nayland Rock—here Eliot would perch himself
On a bench and take in the gunmetal sea
Watch the locals whelking

'On Margate Sands. / I can connect/
Nothing with nothing. / The broken finger nails
of dirty hands. / My people humble people
people who expect/ Nothing'.

To the east—'the scotched brown cliffs'

Meanwhile *Mauberley* received another mauling

O Aboulie
'lack of will'

jellied eels

'On distinctive quad-ruled paper that he
had borrowed from Pound, Eliot produced
a heavily worked pencil manuscript
of seventeen lines in couplets, a portrait
of a patron of the arts, Lady Katzegg'

Venus Anadyomene

Dry Salvages

'Drinking water was contaminated, the gaff jaws
jammed, the garboard-strake leaking, the crew gonorrhoeal'

Eliot had so long been "overworked and almost
permanently separated from his craving – 'poetical
composition' – which had induced 'a frantic state of mind"

First Remembrance Day:
'red paper flowers were sold along the pier'

The great fatigue
Exhaustedly thumbing through
The pages of Mar gate

Frag
men
ts

¶

* 9 7 8 1 8 3 8 4 9 6 6 7 8 *

BV - #0101 - 140624 - C0 - 234/156/11 - CC - 9781838496678 - Gloss Lamination